Rations and Romance

C000132744

York in the
Second World War

Van Wilson

Published by York Archaeological Trust 2008
47 Aldwark, York YO1 7BX
www.yorkarchaeology.co.uk

Designed and typeset by Lesley Collett, York Archaeological Trust
Cover design by Lesley Collett

Printed by B&B Press, Rotherham

ISBN No. 978-1-874454-42-7

CONTENTS

PREFACE

The Second World War, from 1939-1945, was a crucial period in York's history. Every citizen was affected by the war, man, woman and child, in one way or another.

Last year York Archaeological Trust produced a new edition of Van Wilson's Hungate oral history book, *'Rich in All But Money; Life in Hungate 1900-1938'*. The Trust is now delighted to have produced a new oral history book by Van Wilson on York during the Second World War.

The book, which again focuses on the local community, follows on from our hugely successful project *Home Front Recall* for which we interviewed a number of people who lived and worked in York during the Second World War. We amassed hours of recordings and dozens of photographs. With this material, and that kindly supplied by York Oral History Society, we have been able to record the experiences of over 70 people who lived in York during the war. From these accounts we learn about life as an evacuee sleeping on shakedowns in the apple loft, parading in the Home Guard and using spiders' webs to make theodolites, as well as experiencing air raids, eating horse meat, dancing in the De Grey Rooms and having tea at Bettys.

These reminiscences, along with the photographic record, give a wonderful insight into life in York during the Second World War. I believe they provide an important third thread to understanding our immediate past, along with the historical and archaeological records with which York Archaeological Trust is more generally associated. There are fewer and fewer men and women who lived through this important period in York's history, and we are very grateful to all of those whose memories have helped to bring the period alive.

John Walker,
Chief Executive,
York Archaeological Trust

INTRODUCTION

In 2005, to commemorate the 60th anniversary of the end of the Second World War, we conducted an oral history project, recording memories of York people who had lived or worked on the home front during the war. Seeing York in World War Two through the eyes of those who remember it, makes for fascinating 'viewing'. The stories of ordinary men and women, who lived through extraordinary times, give us glimpses into that world, where life had to be 'lived today', because the possibility of death was never far away. Pain, fear and loss feature in these reminiscences but they are tempered with humour, with matter-of-factness, with the sense that people were pulling together towards a common goal.

The firemen and air raid wardens who dug out the women and children trapped under two or three storeys of rubble; the members of the Home Guard, training long hours in their determination to protect their country; the families who took in other people's children to keep them safe from the bombing; the women in factories making munitions, handling dangerous materials and often doing what had been 'men's work'; the girls ploughing and working on the land to increase the nation's food production; the observers and gunners seeking to defend the cities and towns; the men and women trying to keep their families fed and, when they managed to acquire a few eggs or a chicken, sharing them with their friends and neighbours; and the performers who travelled around providing music and entertainment to lift the spirits and increase morale — are all represented here.

One lady commented, "We didn't do anything special, we just got on with it", and that seems to sum up the views of those we interviewed. Their courage in the face of adversity, and their care for their fellow human beings shine through. It has been a real privilege to share the memories of those who are featured here, to meet those who lived through a period which changed the world forever. By allowing us to record their memories, they are ensuring that these stories, this 'living history' will be kept for future generations.

Van Wilson
March 2008

v

*Some of the interviewees who contributed to this book
at a celebration held at the Yorkshire Air Museum, Elvington, 2006
to mark the end of the **Home Front Recall** project
sponsored by the Imperial War Museum and the Heritage Lottery Fund.*

Back row, left to right: *Harold Welburn, Gordon Fenwick, John Scott, Jack Turner, Keith Turner, Gerald Barker, Tony Wood, Peter Binns, Alwyn Banks, Bob Ferguson, Tony Jerrum, Frank Jackson, John Jessop.*
Middle row, left to right: *Jean Cayley, Avril Appleton, Lois Wilson, Evelyn Hudson.*
Front row, left to right: *Mary Beilby, Mildred Veal, Brenda Milner, Kate Houghton, Sheila White, Rubye Readhead, Joyce Elliott, Maureen Jerrum.*

CHAPTER ONE

PREPARING FOR WAR

After the First World War, the Treaty of Versailles imposed severe penalties on Germany. The country was not allowed to have an army or air force, and had to pay a huge sum in war damages. The 1920s and early '30s saw an economic depression throughout the world, with Germany in particular in a state of collapse. When Adolf Hitler came to power in 1933, he was welcomed as a strong leader who promised to get the country back on its feet. But his ambition knew no bounds, something which the ordinary citizens did not realise at first. He contravened the treaty and rearmed the nation, reoccupied the Rhineland and defied the rest of Europe. It was clear that he was 'on the move'.

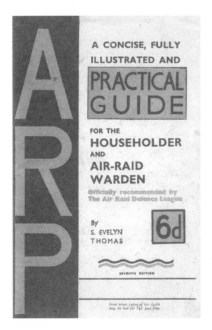

ARP guide issued to homes in York

Preparations for war in this country really began as long ago as 1935 when the government set aside £100,000 to implement ARP (Air Raid Precautions). The bombing which had occurred in the First World War took England by surprise, and during the 1920s and '30s, the Home Office commissioned studies into the possible effect of air raids on this country. After the Spanish Civil War in 1936, when the world saw the power of the German Luftwaffe, the government knew that air raids on the UK would have an enormous impact. A study in 1938 suggested that there could be as many as 3,500 tons of bombs dropped in a single day, with 175,000 casualties.

From 1936 onwards, classes were held locally for the instruction of the general public in 'anti gas' and ARP. In 1937, the government passed the Air Raid Precautions Act, which put the onus on local authorities to draw up plans in the event of war, and implement them. In March 1937, the York Corporation had started to look at what large buildings in the city might be appropriate to use for casualties. The Social Hall on Huntington Road estate, amongst others, was earmarked to be used as a 'casualty clearing station in case of air raids'. A year later in March 1938, Lt Col Victor Daly was appointed as city ARP Officer at a salary of £400 p.a. By April, Daly had an office at 32 Parliament Street, with two clerks. Lectures on air raid precautions took place, and by July, several ARP wardens' posts were being erected. There had to be training in the use of gas masks, and how to deal with bombs. By mid 1938, 200,000 people throughout the country had signed up as ARP wardens.

In the same year, Hitler moved into Austria, and later invaded Czechoslovakia. The British Prime Minister, Neville Chamberlain, met with Hitler and the French and Italian premiers in Munich on 30th September, and returned waving a piece of paper and proclaiming, "Peace in our time", and many people sighed with relief. But their optimism was short-lived.

From 1938, York, like many other cities in England, took in refugees from various parts of Europe. A hostel for male Czech refugees opened on Acomb Road, with 27 men initially. The men got work cultivating market gardens at the York Settlement, (founded in 1909 by Arnold Rowntree to provide adult education in the city), with some being taken on by farmers. The females who came, including some German Jews, but also Czech and Suedetenland refugees, were placed as domestics in various homes. 84 men and nine wives were billeted in the town, and had a social club and English lessons at the Settlement. They were given free passes to the theatre for Monday evenings and passes to the city slipper baths. The men had shoe and clothes repairing classes and the women sewing. York people gave gifts to equip the hostels where they stayed. But emigration from much of Europe stopped when war was declared.

At this time, the York Chief Constable, Harry Herman, began to make arrangements for sirens from the First World War to be put in place, and two additional ones were purchased for Clifton and outside the Beeswing public house on Hull Road. The next step was to provide air raid shelters. In January 1939, trenches were dug and shelters built in the moat at Station Avenue (to hold 165 people but later extended to 345), Kent Street (for 225 but later extended to 360), Lord Mayor's Walk (for 100 initially but later extended) and Scarcroft Stray (for 239). Above-ground shelters in 14 inch brick were constructed at St George's Field to hold 400, Merchant Adventurer's Garden for 400, Leeman Road recreational ground for 1200, Leeman Road itself for 1000, the Museum Gardens for 400 and Castlegate School for 200. £25,000 was borrowed from outside the city to construct shelters at York schools, which would be repayable over ten years. The city was divided into 13 wards. Eventually there were four public shelters in the Acomb ward, seven in Bootham and Huntington Road, five in Clifton including the football ground, five in Fishergate/Fulford Road, six in Heworth and Tang Hall, five in Holgate, four in the Knavesmire area, five in Mickle-gate Ward, three in Monkgate Ward, four in the Scarcroft area, five in Walmgate Ward, sixteen in the Castlegate Ward which included part of the city centre, and twenty in the Guildhall Ward, stretching from Micklegate to Coney Street and up to the City Library. The shelter at Baile Hill was the biggest with space for 1200.

As well as the threat of gas and heavy explosive bombs, the government was also expecting the lighter incendiary bombs, which would not explode but would start fires. A heavy bomber could carry 1000 of these. In April 1939, the Home Office allocated 110 stirrup hand pumps for the air raid wardens' posts, to be used for incendiaries. Several people remember having a card which read SP in their window, alerting their neighbours that they had a stirrup pump. An auxiliary fire service made up of volunteers was established to support the main fire brigade, with eight sub stations.

In July, Hunter and Smallpage, in Goodramgate, supplied and fixed dark blinds to the Guildhall and Municipal (Council) Offices at a cost of £79.10s.9d. A city blackout trial was pronounced a success and large stores of blackout curtains were obtained by shopkeepers. On 25th August, the press reported that 'peace hangs by a thread and only Hitler will cut it', but the following day, all Germans were preparing to leave England.

An information and recruiting bureau was established at the city library, and a Head Air Raid Warden appointed for each of the 13 wards. There were four main first aid posts, plus two mobile ones. Each of them had a medical officer and a staff nurse available. The one based at Lendal Repository, had Dr Reginald Dench, the father of actress Judi Dench, as its doctor.

Women learn to use stirrup pump, Nunmill Street (York Oral History Society)

Sandbags were placed in front of what were considered important buildings. A number of voluntary Czech labourers were brought in to fill the sandbags, and were given an allowance of sixpence each a day for cigarettes.

August 21st to 28th was designated ARP week. Advertisements appeared asking for 1520 more volunteers aged between 18 and 65. These were to comprise 520 air raid wardens, 300 evacuation workers, 229 territorials, 127 for first aid parties, 100 auxiliary nurses, 93 special constables, 81 auxiliary firemen and 70 for the National Defence Company.

On 2nd September, the day before war was declared, a broadcast urged people to obtain dark material for their windows. But shops were unable to cope with the demand, and within half an hour of the broadcast, the whole stock of 1000 rolls of black wallpaper was sold by a large York shop. The shop manager went off to the mill to obtain more rolls and could only get 120. These were bought by customers in three minutes! People were then advised to put up white paper and paint it black. Motorists received information about the government's emergency lighting regulations and the council had to organise how to switch off street lighting.

As well as the large public air raid shelters, there was also the distribution of home shelters. The city had ordered 15,000. Any family with an income under £250 was entitled to a shelter by the government. Others could purchase one. Alwyn Banks explains,

There were three types of shelter, the Morrison, indoors, the Anderson, corrugated iron in [the shape of an] *archway, and then, like we had in Eldon Terrace, a brick built one with a concrete roof. Ours had electricity in 'cos I was an electrician. And it had a bunk in, 'cos if I had to get up in the night for an air raid, and go in, I'd get into the bunk and go to sleep and stay there till morning. I wouldn't bother to go back into the house. That was still there when my mum and dad died, up to maybe 12 years ago.*

He became an apprentice electrician and was also involved with ARP. One of his tasks was to check the lighting in the public shelters.

The shelters had a flight of steps down and an archway going in, then the tunnel ran along and then another flight of steps to come out at the other end. When I went down, instead of turning right along the tunnel, I would go to the left. There was a little alcove area where all the switches were and a box with the batteries in. Presumably one of the local air raid wardens, if a siren went, would go down and switch the lights on, so at least the people could come down and walk along in light.

Mavis Morton recalls receiving an air raid shelter.

My father grew beautiful chrysanthemums, and within about a week of war, they were coming round with these big sheets of corrugated iron to build your air raid shelter. My mother and father were always arguing, and then one night, at two in the morning, I could hear my mother going on and on and she was saying, "Get the shelter up", and he was saying, "I want to finish my prize chrysanthemums first". But the argument got out of hand, and me father got out of bed at two o'clock in the morning and started digging his prize chrysanthemums up.

On 24th September, 84,300 civilian respirators were received from Leeds, and taken to be stored at the Tramways Depot in Fulford. Rowntree's and Sessions, the printers, undertook to make boxes for them. It was expected that air raids would result in many casualties, and the city had to be equipped to deal with them. A control head-quarters was set up in the basement of the Guildhall with equipment and staff. Mortuaries had to be put in place. JJ Hunt's disused brewing factory in Aldwark was commandeered for that purpose in September

Alwyn Banks 2005 (Van Wilson)

Alwyn Banks in RAF c1944.
(Alwyn Banks)

1939. It cost £120 to convert, and the Cattle Market butter shed was converted for the same purpose at a more modest cost of £35. The Racing Stables at Dringhouses were also used. There were extra ambulances needed, a hospital supplies depot, a decontamination team and a team to defuse unexploded bombs, as well as rescue parties. The ARP officer based at the Guildhall was allowed to use the Smoke Room for his work, provided no meetings were being held at the time.

Many companies, schools, shops and other businesses had their own firewatchers on a rota basis. Sometimes they were on the roof of the building, otherwise they would patrol around the premises. Extra telephones had to be available for emergencies. Builders, joiners, plumbers and electricians had to be engaged to work on various aspects of the preparations, and back-up office staff were employed. One very important aspect was the requisitioning of large buildings for evacuees, the billeting of refugees and members of the forces. There were also emergency rest and feeding centres to be set up, to feed and help the homeless. Units of the Home Guard were formed and trained to defend the city. Traffic direction signs and signs at the railway station had to be taken down or masked. Sufficient petrol supplies had to be available for transport relating to the war effort.

Sheila Goater recalls,

When the war started, they issued us all with gas masks which we had to carry about, in little square cardboard boxes with a string to go round your neck or shoulder. You were supposed to carry them with you everywhere you went. When you were at school, they sent you home to get it if you forgot to take it. Gradually they produced fancy holders for these gas masks, it made it more glamorous. We used to get air raid sirens but nothing happened at all here for a long time.

Sheila Goater 2007 (Lesley Collett)

Sheila Goater as young woman (Sheila Goater)

I used to travel every day to Leeds. I don't remember the trains being affected. I went on the bus mostly. You didn't go on holiday much. The seaside places, you couldn't go on the sands, they had barbed wire on them to prevent invasion. When I was at school there always used to be a lot of buses parked just outside the station. We used to call them invasion buses. I think we really thought there was going to be an invasion, when the war started. All sorts of things in wartime get put in place and there's no explanation given, you aren't supposed to ask. Presumably they had plans for evacuation if it was necessary. I don't think we thought that far about what we'd do, we'd never been invaded in this country.

Kate Houghton was a child when the war began.

I lived in Hampden Street, off Low Priory Street, and our shelter was under the Bar Walls, all the way along from Victoria Bar to Dewsbury Terrace. That was where we went when the siren called. It was all railinged along and so they came and took all the railings off. They were used for the war effort. There were at least two flights of stone stairs down. My father was an air raid warden, once he did get blown down the stairs. He was okay, but the blast!

The shelter had benches on both sides and we used to often live down there for hours, wrapped up well and possibly with something to eat. There were quite a few of us children around. I just remember it was cold. There was no heating. We tried to be cheerful, but it wasn't very pleasant when you were hearing bombs. There was an unexploded bomb at Cooke, Troughton and Sims, which was an armaments factory near us. We were all evacuated that time into the shelter, as they thankfully defused it. But that was a bit dicey.

My mother hadn't anyone but me at home and she had to take in two girls that worked at the armaments. They lived at Pocklington. She always had lodgers. I think there were about three men came after Ivy and Dorothy left. She had to provide breakfast and an evening meal.

Mary Barnes remembers,

You had to be trained about gas masks. We had to go to Foss Islands Road to a building there, they had various different kinds of gases. You had lectures on them. There was one that burnt you and chlorine gas and all the things that they could do, and if you were called upon you had to do the first aid. I don't think they ever used gas in England.

The York artist Robert Robinson designed a flower bed on the bar walls moat near Leeman Road arch in 1939, which showed the ARP badge, and the words, 'A City Prepared, A City Spared'. It was felt that the city was as well equipped as it could be for what lay ahead.

Yorkshire Evening Press

CHAPTER TWO

THE EVACUEES

Before war was declared, the government advised parents to evacuate their children from the cities into rural parts of the country, or even abroad. Over one and a half million left in the first few days of September 1939, and normal services at London's stations were suspended to allow for this mass transportation. They were mostly schoolchildren, but also pregnant women and mothers with babies. The government, without looking at it in personal terms, saw the process as a brilliantly executed exercise in logistics, (with the code name Operation Pied Piper), but not perhaps the social and emotional problems which would result.

The photographs of large numbers of children at the stations, wearing school uniforms, clutching a small case and sometimes a teddy bear, the obligatory gas mask in its cardboard box, and a label attached to them, are heart-rending, as are the accounts written by evacuees telling of loneliness, bullying and even abuse. But others describe a joyful and positive experience when friendships were forged which continued long after the war. Whether happy or sad, it is clear that the experience was very significant, and one which the evacuees recall in detail more than 60 years later.

As early as January 1939, the Minister of Health requested a survey of the country to ascertain what accommodation would be available if children were evacuated out of the 'danger zones'. In York, the Town Clerk was instructed to point out the dangers of the city in the event of hostile aircraft invading the country and suggested that the city should not be used to evacuate children. Later that month 72 teachers volunteered to help in taking a census to find out who had rooms available, and this was completed in March. The result was that 26,805 evacuees could be accommodated. In June, the Minister told the city that he could not 'see our way to release York from its liability as a receiving area under the Government Evacuation Scheme'. An Evacuation Committee was set up consisting of the Lord Mayor, two councillors and two representatives from the Education Committee. Householders were told that they must take evacuees if they had the space. In September, 60 small children from local children's homes were sent to Hovingham Lodge, which was owned by Sir William Worsley, under the care of mostly voluntary staff. It was agreed by the Public Assistance Committee, that they would pay twelve shillings per child per week for children aged two to four years sent to the evacuation centre there, as well as the cost of providing a probationer nurse.

Fourteen centres were set up in York for dealing with evacuees, each having a supervisor and a staff of about 40, including the actual billeting officers. The city purchased 2,400 blankets for the centres, as well as catering equipment. Each centre was given a different colour, for example the Holgate centre was mauve, the Fishergate salmon and the Knavesmire was magenta.

The evacuees who came to the York area in early September totalled 1826 school age children with teachers and helpers, and 1846 children under five and their mothers. As well as reception officers, there were also assistants, medical officers and first aid workers in place to receive them. They came to Haxby and Strensall stations, just outside York, with the reception centres for each village at the school, the Sunday school, the Village Institute and the Methodist Chapel. Each evacuee had been given food rations of one can of meat, two cans of milk, one pound of biscuits and a quarter pound of chocolate. Host families were paid 10/6d a week for each evacuee. The children were told to bring their gas mask, change of underclothing, night clothes, house shoes or plimsolls, socks or stockings, toothbrush, towel, handkerchiefs and a warm coat.

Tony and Maureen Jerrum both lived in Haxby as children, and their families took in evacuees. Tony remembers,

We had evacuees from Middlesborough, about my age, nine or ten. They just fitted in and we enjoyed their company. Some were with us just a week, then they moved. They got off the train and they'd be assembled in the schoolyard and it was convenient for them to go to Mrs Jerrum's [a stopping off point] for a few days. They'd get homesick. We played games to help them, football and cricket.

Tony and Maureen Jerrum later in the war
(T & M Jerrum)
Tony and Maureen Jerrrum 2005 (Mike Race)

Evacuees weren't used to the type of food that we used to eat. New pota-toes and vegetables all came out of the back garden, and runner beans. They'd probably never had them before.

Maureen recalls,

Tony's mother used to make and knit clothes. She knitted a cardigan in a day and a half. She knitted 15 pixie hoods and she taught the children to knit, they knitted their own balaclavas and mittens. We knitted socks for the army as well. [Schools provided wool for children to knit for the forces]. We'd play dominoes and that would teach them numbers. There wasn't a lot of toys but a lot of love and caring.

[In our family] *we only had one girl, Ann. We had to sleep top and tail at night time, as there were aleady five of us girls. We had two double beds and we slept across. The headboard was actually against the wall. When Ann came to us, grandma gave us plucked feathers from the birds on the farm to go in the pillows. We never had pillow cases.*

She didn't want to go home in the end. Quite a few stayed on. They got to be 14 and got chance to work in the area.

Maureen Jerrum in uniform
(T & M Jerrum)

Avril Appleton was evacuated to the city from Hull.

Avril Appleton 2005 (Mike Race)

We actually came the day before war was declared. I can just remember all assembling in the school with our gas masks. I was five and I hadn't started school, so my mother was allowed to come with me and also my brother who was two years older. And all I remember was a long train journey. My mother was convinced we were going to Scotland because it was so long on the train. I think we arrived at Haxby first. They said it was York, but it could have been John O'Groats, we seemed to have been hours and hours on that train. We were given a meal at Haxby and then sent to different areas. A group of us went to Clifton Without, outside the city boundary. I don't think York city itself had any, most evacuees went to Clifton, Osbaldwick, New Earswick, all those villages. I remember we were in this hall and allocated billets. We seemed to be the last because lots of people wanted me but they didn't want my mother. But they took my brother, he went on his own, he got in with a nice family, they worked at Rowntree's. I just remember walking through the streets, we finally got this billet and it was a young couple and they had a baby which I thought would be rather nice. But we had to sleep on the floor and I remember my mother crying that night, and the next day we were back to the billeting officer.

We seemed to be always moving billets because there was always something that didn't suit my mother. I think the main problem was two women in one kitchen. And one house, they only gave us bully beef, corned beef, that was off the ration, but she was convinced that they were having better food than us, like tins of salmon and other delicacies. And she made me go and look in the dustbin to see what they'd

Evacuees arrive at Canon Lee School, Clifton, September 1939. Avril Appleton's mother is on back row in white beret, and Avril is in front of her, fringe and ribbon showing. (Avril Appleton)

been eating. I remember having to sneak out when nobody was looking. I must have seen some tins of something because the next day we were back again to the billeting officer. It all came to a head one morning when I was having my breakfast in this lady's house. And it was puffed wheat and I can see it now, this lady was cleaning the grate out and all of a sudden she started getting on at me and saying, "Your daughter makes such a noise". So mother said, "That's it, I've had enough, we're going back to Hull". And so we went back to Hull. But we hadn't got back long and the Blitz started in Hull so we were sent off to an aunt in a village near Goole. Then, 'cos my father was a fireman on the railway, he was given promotion to be an engine driver. And he could come either to Darlington or York and he chose York and he lived in lodgings for a while before we all moved in 1942. And as children, we said to my dad, "Oh let's go to York", because we'd heard of Rowntree's chocolates. We thought we might get a chance of having some!

The first few months of the war were christened 'the phoney war' as there were none of the anticipated air raids and the country seemed very quiet. This resulted in a number of the evacuees returning home during the early months of 1940. However later that year, after the defeat of Dunkirk, and the Battle of Britain which took place in the air above southern England, large numbers of evacuees were sent away again. Many travelled overseas, on board ships to parts of what was then the British Empire, including Canada, South Africa, Australia and New Zealand. Some were sent to relatives or friends, but many had to move in with strangers. Before the children left, their parents had to sign a waiver releasing the government of all responsibility for the child's welfare!

In July 1940, there were plans to evacuate children from children's homes to Canada, New Zealand and Australia under the government's scheme for evacuation of unaccompanied school children for the duration of the war. A board was set up of prominent men and women to oversee the scheme and similar bodies set up overseas to take charge of the children as soon as they arrived there. The process seemed to be successful until 16th September 1940 when the ship *City of Benares*, sailing from Liverpool to Canada, was torpedoed and sunk, with 80 children and 200 adults dying as a result. It was a great shock to the country. The ship should have been escorted during the crossing but its escorts left it exposed too soon. Even the German submarine crew who sank it, wept themselves when they heard that the vessel was full of children being evacuated. Because of this disaster, the government immediately stopped the overseas evacuation scheme.

In 2005, 60 years after the conflict ended, hundreds of evacuees had their first official reunion, as they marched together through the streets of London for a service in Westminster Abbey, and the Evacuees Reunion Association was formed. A wreath in memory of the children from the SS *Benares* was taken by the navy to be dropped into the Atlantic.

Gerald Barker 2005 (Van Wilson)

A York man who spent the war overseas is Gerald Barker. The youngest of three brothers, he and his second eldest brother Ted were sent to Canada for the whole six years of war. The experience had a great impact on Gerald, even though it was only for a relatively short period of his life. But they were formative years. He kept in touch with many of the people he met whilst in Canada and he still has a framed photograph of the family house in Nova Scotia on his wall.

We left about August 1940. I think with my father catching the tail end of the First World War, he realised what a power they had been. He really thought we might be over-run, and it would be better to have two sons away from the country if possible, which is what happened. There were various families from York on the ship, which funnily enough was called the Duchess of York, *built I think in the '20s and a stocky ship, not that comfortable. But it got us over to Canada safely.* [The ship was a Canadian Pacific ocean liner built in 1928, converted into a troopship in 1940 and in 1943 was attacked and sunk off the coast of Morocco].

We were to have landed in Montreal, but found ourselves in Halifax, Nova Scotia. It took ten days because although we left York in early August, we were then sent up to Glasgow where we had to wait for the convoy to assemble. We were up there for about a week, then we went out into the Atlantic, which was beginning to be a rather dangerous place. There were numerous destroyers, other merchantmen and HMS Hood, [the famous battle cruiser, which was later sunk on 24 May 1941], *with us for quite some while. It took ten days in all to cross, and*

Gerald Barker (in centre) with brothers Ted and Denzil (who was in the RAF). Nova Scotia, Canada 1943. (Gerald Barker)

as the days went by, as it got safer in the mid Atlantic or just beyond, the convoy dispersed in another direction. I think even though I was only nine at the time, you felt it was for your own good, it was for your safety and well-being long-term.

The people we went to were the McKays, they were of Scottish descent. It was very beneficial to my brother and myself to be kept together. Mrs McKay was born in 1880, she was old enough to be my grandmother. It was a very large house, and the part of the house which we were using, there was just Mr and Mrs McKay, my brother and myself, and they did take in a girl to do the housekeeping and cooking. The upper part was a highways department office from which Mr McKay used to look after the three counties of Nova Scotia's highways.

It was a lovely house, not typical necessarily in size because they were probably one of the more wealthy families. It was an adventure at that time, it was a comfortable existence and so I think homesickness didn't come into it too much. We arrived after dark. It was a long haul from Halifax to Clyde River. I was having trouble with my smallpox inoculation, and it caused such a bad reaction to it, it was recommended that I didn't start school straightaway. It was a little school, two rooms with five grades in each room, with only two teachers.

You could send a telegram home once a month, it was usually a pre-worded thing, just to let them know that you were okay. I would say in general it was a comfortable home, they were a caring couple even though they might have that grandparent image. The first Christmas we got a sledge each and skates and oddly enough Mark's the toymakers, the American firm, were making tanks that spit out something, looking as if it was fire. We got a little train set, very sturdy thing, we brought it home in actual fact. And always sweets, candies and things like that.

For Gerald, the problem was not being evacuated. He quickly settled in. But coming back was not easy, settling back into a different way of life again.

I think one of the problems for me was the change from their education system, even down to the money system being decimalised, and coming back to pounds, shillings and pence, which seemed almost foreign by the time five years had elapsed. I did an 'O' level in French and realised how little French I had actually done in Canada itself. That's strange really because Nova Scotia is full of French villages. Most everywhere had little white fences, even down in Nova Scotia. The reason people were fenced off was possibly because every other family would keep a cow. There was no rationing, of course. Mr McKay had some land ploughed up opposite the house. We were self sufficient in vegetables. You could grow tomatoes outside, and sweetcorn, squash, pumpkin and

Gerald Barker on left, with brother Ted and Mrs McKay 1943, Nova Scotia. (Gerald Barker)

potatoes. It was my first introduction to Colorado potato beetle. My job was to flick the leaves off the potatoes, pick the leaves with eggs on and dump them in kerosene.

I know that Mrs McKay enjoyed having a couple of boys in her household, provided you toed the line and did things in the way that you should, because I know my chores on a Saturday were going through the house and cleaning and dusting a bit, that sort of thing. And I used to get up and make some pretty stodgy porridge for Mr McKay, and start the morning coffee off.

Gerald went back to Canada 20 years later, when Mr McKay was 80 years old. But by that time Mrs McKay had died. He recalls their parting in 1945 and says he understands now how it must have been like a bereavement for her and for all those who acted as surrogate parents.

I know that Mrs McKay insisted on staying in her hotel until she could see the ship actually going out to sea. I learned a lot from her, she was really first class in so many ways, a valuable person to my life. Someone said, "We all need our mentors", and I was glad of her being such for me even though I might not have gone in the direction she wished for me.

Mary Beilby was born in 1918, at the end of the First World War, in Lincolnshire. When war began she was a children's nurse in what was known as the workhouse, but then she moved to Newburgh Priory School to be matron, before she married and came to York.

We didn't get much bombing at Newburgh. It's right in the country, just next to Coxwold. You'd hardly have known there was a war on there except that we had to worry about the blackouts. There was three schools. They were all evacuated [to Newburgh]. One was Pannal Ash from Harrogate and one from Southend on Sea and then some local children that were paid for, because it was a private school.

I was in charge of 92 children. I had an assistant matron and another lady that used to help. It was all boys, we'd some at three and a half, up to about 19. It was a private place but the parents wanted them to come because they were worrying about the bombing. We'd quite a lot of teachers but they were mostly elderly 'cos all the young ones were called up. They'd come back out of retirement. We used to go long walks 'cos it was all country round there. And we used to play various games, cricket, rounders and all sorts of things. We used to make them as happy as we could.

Rose Wilcox 2004 (Rose Wilcox)

Rose Wilcox as young woman (Rose Wilcox)

Rose Mary Wilcox, who has lived in York for many years, actually came from Leeds, and during the war was evacuated to Pateley Bridge.

My mum said we were going on a long holiday and that was the first time I'd heard about evacuation. And that was with my sister. She was six years older, she'd be ten or eleven.

We were all assembled on Leeds station. There seemed to be hundreds and hundreds of people, and crying mums. One or two mums went with them but my mum didn't. We had some teachers that went with us. I can remember all of us having luggage labels tied to our jerseys or coats. We had carrier bags or pillow cases with our stuff in and a cardboard box with our gasmasks in, around our shoulders. We were taken into this big hall and told to sit cross-legged on the floor. It was a bit like a cattle market after that because the various people who were going to have evacuees came in and picked out the ones they wanted. A few scruffy little lads with runny noses were the last to be picked, and one or two families of children. We were lucky because we were kept together, and we went to a farm right at the top of the dale. It was quite remote for us after living in Leeds. We were on shakedowns in the apple loft. I've never seen so many apples. That's the first time I had warm milk straight from a cow. Our supper that first night was two slices of crusty homemade bread and milk straight from the dairy, different again to the milk you get in bottles.

It was a very busy farm. I think they had three or four sons that seemed real old to me but they'd have only been in their twenties. I suppose she had a husband as well. She never stopped. She used to get up very early and she used to bake and work on the farm and work in the garden, and I suppose farmers' wives are very busy people. My sister was expected to help in the dairy and the kitchen when we weren't at school.

I don't remember being hungry. They used to have a lot of rabbit stew. They kept sheep and pigs. I quite liked the pigs, I couldn't think after they'd had them so long, that they could eat them, but they did. It was wonderful for us to go and look in the pig pen and see the baby piglets. And we probably had pork at the weekend but it never occurred to us that it might have been one of the piglets that we'd been looking at. In a way I think it did a lot of the kids good if you got to somewhere that was all right. We used to hear various tales in the village of kids that had gone to other farms and they weren't as lucky as we were.

We used to go to school on a shire horse, four of us sat on the back, my sister and me and two kids who were fairly close. I think it would be two or three miles down into school and we used to go on this big shaggy horse which was the first time I'd ever got close to a horse as big as that. We'd take a medicine bottle full of milk and a sandwich, or a little flat cake. And that was our lunch.

We might as well have been on the Planet Zog 'cos the war didn't seem to affect us. You were miles away from anywhere, they'd have had a job to find a farm from up there. I don't think we ever thought about bombs. Even in Pateley Bridge itself, they might have had planes passing over but I don't think they got any bomb damage.

It was a bit lonely especially at the weekend. We were used to having corner shops and popping out, if any visitors came they'd give you tuppence for spice, as they called it, which were sweets. And there wasn't anything like that, we were stuck in the middle of nowhere. The highlight of our week was chapel, over about six fields. And hail, rain or snow, we went to chapel. It was all a bit strange. To us it was like going back in time because we were townies and they were village people.

We made friends but the village kids weren't very friendly towards us and they looked on us as outsiders. We were told it was for the duration but we didn't know what the duration meant. The family weren't lovey dovey but they weren't cruel. I think we were just an inconvenience more than anything.

Because Leeds didn't get a lot of attention from the Luftwaffe, my mum decided to bring us home. We'd been there probably seven or eight months. We never did get a proper bed, we slept in the apple loft. Looking back I think they were straw pallets with blankets across. I don't like apples even now. Something about it, the smell of an apple, I can go right back to the apple loft.

Mollie Caffrey was born in 1927 in the North East. She was evacuated to Elvington near York, and stayed there after the war.

I came on the 10th September, exactly a week after war broke out. We were told on the Friday at school. We didn't know where we were coming. I had three sisters younger than me. I was 11, Jeannie was 5, Joyce would be 10 and Ivy 8. We were all separated. Joyce and Ivy went

further up the village and I went to the other end with my youngest
sister. Then my father came to fetch them, they couldn't stick it out,
they used to cry themselves to sleep at night.

We were right outside the village, up past the aerodrome. I'd to carry
Jean down to school because she was tiny. Quite often we were late
because we used to play on the way down and watch squirrels and all
sorts. I came to this little tiny village school. What they were doing I'd
done years previously, so I really didn't do much at all. I passed a schol-
arship to go to grammar school, I'd got me uniform and everything.
The parson then, Mr Jackson, he moved heaven and earth to get me to
Mill Mount [Grammar] *School. But the person I was billeted with said,*
"No you can't go, 'cos I can't take Jean to school". So I had to stay and
that's the big regret about coming to Elvington. But I liked the country-
side. My other two sisters were typical town kids. Joyce said, "How you
live in that village, I'll never know. It's like the back of beyond".

But you used to have film shows in Sutton [a nearby village]*, and*
there were dances in the village hall, and tennis and things like that.
The dances were very lively, there was the Free French there and a
lot of Algerians. The air force blokes were after the village girls and
the village boys didn't like it. We used to hear the bombers going out
at night. And listen for them coming back in the early hours of the
morning. You could tell how many left and how many came back.

But I liked it, I stayed in Elvington with the people we were evacuated
with. They moved to Allerthorpe near Pocklington, and he took over
the War Agriculture Committee and I worked for him. Then I went out
with Dennis and stayed and got married.

A lot of people took in unofficial evacuees, distant relatives or friends.
Mary Barnes's family took in friends of her husband's aunt from
London.

They liked it here. After the big air raid of 1942, we had several minor raids, but nothing to what they were having. They'd managed during the heavy bombing but they got absolutely cheesed off with living in shelters all the time. When the flying bombs started, they couldn't take anymore. They asked my husband's aunt if she knew anywhere they could go to escape. She wrote to ask if they could come here. There was Mr and Mrs Elton and their two daughters. Mr Elton had to work during the week, he came up as often as he could. But the womenfolk were here for about two years until 1944. They were very grateful because they could have a rest here.

Doreen Varrie remembers,

My friend lived in Acomb. Her cousin came up from Plymouth. She was only a little girl, she'd be about five. She slept on two orange boxes, made into a bed for her, padded, in a bedroom with my friend. It was so bad in Plymouth. It was relatively peaceful in York. Aunt Annie and Stan used to come up from Edgware in London and my cousin came to stay, Betty from Hull. She slept in our bed, with Pat [her sister] and I. It was a great big bedroom, that front room at Thorpe Street.

In August 1944, nearly 2000 evacuees came to York to escape the 'flying bombs'. In fact 17,000 left London during that month. These were mostly women and children. An 85-year-old lady called Eliza Slade arrived in York on a stretcher, with nine other elderly people. She was clutching a handbag and a black umbrella, all she had left. She had no shoes on, they had gone up with the rest when the flying bomb destroyed her home in London. They were taken to Linton Lodge in Clifton, which had been taken over by the Ministry of Health and turned into a convalescent home. One lady, Jane Harvey, had been bombed out of her home twice, and her remaining belongings looted from the removal van.

One good thing that came out of evacuation was that the process high-lighted the deprivation and ignorance of the children from slum areas, and after the war, social and public welfare became very important, as Mary Barnes says,

The greatest thing that came after the war was the Health Service and the new Education Act 1944, where children had a chance, even if you were working class, to get on. My children benefited from that, they both managed to get scholarships and both went to college. It came to light during the war, all the distress, and they really had to do something about it.

CHAPTER THREE
CIVIL DEFENCE

The task of defending Britain was going to be a tough one. There were two ways, either actively through the armed forces, or passively through what was known as civil defence. Well before war was declared, the government had asked for volunteers, and men and women came together in large numbers ready to make their mark.

The cost of civil defence was partly funded by the Home Office, but local rates were also increased. In York the rate jumped from 1/6d to 2s in the pound, which was quite steep for the time. By 1942, there were 2554 full-time and part-time personnel enrolled in civil defence, as well as police, fire and welfare services.

Rowntree's ARP badge (York Oral History Society)

THE ARP (AIR RAID PRECAUTIONS) SERVICE

The Hawkhills Estate in Easingwold near York was purchased by the War Department in 1937 as one of the two Civil Defence training establishments in the country. The other one was Falfield. They were known as ARP Schools, and were designed for training instructors. This ended in December 1944, but the Hawkhills College is still used for government training today.

On 9th August 1939, the Civil Defence Act stated that employers with more than 30 workers had to report to the local authority what measures were being taken to organise the ARP services and their training. By April 1940,

29

the Foss Islands ARP depot was running well. The members received two meals a day, for three 24 hour shifts. Some slept at the depot and filled the spare time with cards, darts, draughts and concerts, making full use of the wireless and piano.

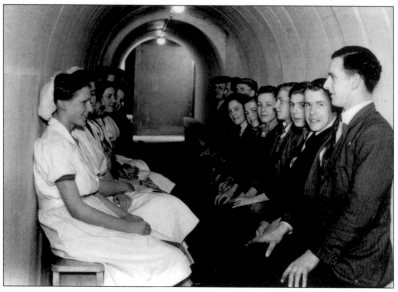

Rowntree's air raid shelter, 1939 (York Oral History Society)

Alwyn Banks worked for the York Corporation as an apprentice electrician. As well as his full-time job, he also helped the ARP service.

Originally the ARP headquarters was in the vaults next to the Guildhall, but they built a special place underground in what is now the car park next to Clifford's Tower. There was a very thick concrete roof. When you went down the steps into it, down the corridor, the first room on the right hand side was where the controller had his office. On the wall was this big map of York, on it were marked red and black dots. The red dots were for all the bombs which had exploded, and the black dots were for unexploded bombs and there was twice as many black dots as red. And on many occasions when they unearthed the bombs and opened them up, there were messages inside from the Czech and Polish slave workers who had deliberately affected the timing or the switching or whatever, so that the bomb didn't go off. It was surprising how many unexploded bombs there were. They were all over the railway shunting yards.

And there were three coloured bulbs, one was green for all clear, one was orange for air raid warning and one was red for imminent alert. The air raid sirens were switched on from there. One of my jobs was to go round them all periodically and oil the mechanisms, so that the shutters worked without them being jammed. The sirens were placed on top of Terry's chocolate factory, Rowntree's Elect block, Acomb School, the Electricity Board in Clifford Street, and the top of the gasometer at Heworth. I used to have to go up there and to go to the top of the gasometer meant going up all the steps on the outside. The top was curved and there was a wooden walkway, and it came to a big round building in the centre, and the gas container rose and fell within the outer shell. The building had a pair of bunks and an electric fire, and was used by fire watchers. They had a telephone down to central head-quarters. The one on top of Rowntree's Elect block overlooked Clifton aerodrome. You could sit up there having oiled the air raid siren and watch the aeroplanes taking off and landing which was very good. It was good fun going up to the top of Rowntree's and Terry's. I was quite happy to do that until I went into the air force.

After the Baedeker Raid in 1942, all the air raid sirens had an addition, an electric motor with a fan at each end. We then put on the cuckoo system, an imminent alert. When the siren sounded, it was a wailing noise because the motor was switched on and off, on and off, so speed picked up and slowed down which gave a wailing sound. It was a continuous note from the siren for imminent alert, as shutters at each end were operated with an electric solenoid, [a loop of wire which produces a magnetic field when an electric current passes through it]. *So a cuckoo sound was made. That was controlled from the ARP headquarters.*

All the underground shelters had 24 volt lighting which was run by electricity off the mains. But it had a change over switch so if bombs knocked out the mains, you could switch it over onto batteries. I used to have to go round and top up all the lead acid batteries and put them on charge, and make sure all the bulbs in the public shelters worked. It wasn't arduous. I'd been involved in installing all this equipment so I knew what it was all about, and it was only a matter of going off for a day cycling round to Terry's, Rowntree's and the gasometer and going up and checking that everything worked. And as far as the underground shelters were concerned, it was a fairly simple job to take a couple of bottles of distilled water on my bike handlebars and go down and check that the batteries were topped up and were being charged. So for a couple of years it was just a nice little sideline job which I could go off and do when I wanted to.

Mary Barnes worked with the ARP service later in the war.

In a strange way, there was always a feeling of excitement, I suppose you never knew what was coming next. A night I remember vividly, it was a gorgeous spring night and all of a sudden the [RAF] bombers started to fly across and they didn't just come in ones and twos that night, there were hundreds came over. We all thought, "Goodness what's going on?" They were going over until late on, then during the early hours of the morning, we heard them limping back. You could tell when something was the matter, they made funny noises. They were coming back in bits and bats until the next day. We heard this was the first thousand bomber raid on Cologne.

I was lucky I didn't have much action on the nights I was on duty. I was very fortunate, our main thing was we used to get warnings if there was an enemy about. We were sort of on the alert but mainly patrolling to see if lights were on. If you did see a light you had to knock on people's doors, "Get your lights out".

The ARP Service needed a lot of messengers, so a number of young people were recruited. Doreen Angus was one of them.

I was at the post at the old Fever Hospital on Yearsley Bridge. I was messenger for the air raid warden there and was issued with a tin hat and gas mask. I remember quite clearly riding this old bike from the Fever Hospital to the Guildhall. My father was a fireman at Rowntree's and we had bells in the house. When we got the yellow warning to say aircraft were on their way, father had to go.

We learned how to use a stirrup pump, and a bucket of sand. We did have a bomber come down in Haley's Terrace, where Rowntree's Theatre is. The bells went, and father rushed out and said, "Go in the shelter and stay there". It was a Polish crew, badly damaged, coming back to East Moor and unfortunately it crashed there. We kept in the shelter that night. We had an Anderson in the garden, and were also allowed to use shelters under the dining hall at Rowntree's, with firemen's wives and children.

Frank Jackson recalls,

There were two people on Beckfield Lane who were air raid wardens. A man and wife, the Hartleys. Father built our own air raid shelter. We used to huddle in there and my mother used to read Grimm's Fairy Tales. Father worked at the Carriageworks. He'd do firewatching so many nights a week and patrol around.

ARP demonstrations were held regularly at the Guildhall as well as wartime cookery lectures in various York schools, and gas and electricity showrooms. But there was some hostility from members of the public towards the air raid wardens and there were frequent readers' letters in the *Yorkshire Evening Press* complaining about their officiousness.

They had to be very vigilant about the blackout, and any offenders were given severe penalties. In the early months of the war, there were large numbers of accidents, including fatalities, due to the blackout regulations. The manager of Leak and Thorpe received two visits from police officers concerning the use of pilot lights in the shop arcade. But when the lights were extinguished, a number of people walked into the shop windows. In October 1939, nationally there were 1130 deaths on the roads due to the blackout. Yet the Chief Constable reported in May 1940, that 'York's blackout is still far from good', and a poster directed people to, 'Black Out or be Bombed Out, Join the ARP at once'.

THE POLICE

In early September 1939, the Home Office instructed local authorities to recruit a Police War Reserve for the duration of the war. On 25th September, the York Watch Committee accepted the tender of Messrs Huggins, Sons & Co of Bristol to supply 150 jackets, trousers and over-coats at a cost of £653.15s, for the War Reserve. Another £46.17s.6d was spent on the supply of 150 caps. The following month, 136 pairs of boots were bought for the police, and 200 mackintoshes for Special Constables. At the same time, sandbags were ordered to protect the police boxes in the city. A number of appropriate buildings, including the Old Red Lion Hotel in Micklegate, had to be converted into auxil-iary police stations for the Police Reserve to use. In November 1939, they were given a bicycle allowance of one shilling each a week.

In July 1940, the pay of War Police reservists was increased to £3.5s a week with an additional proficiency pay of five shillings a week. Messrs Huggins were again given the order for uniforms, and provided serge patrol jackets and cloth trousers for one superintendent, six inspectors, and cloth trousers for 130 sergeants and constables, at a total cost of £220.2s.3d.

From the very beginning of the war, there was pressure on the police force to employ women. In July 1940, the York branch of the National Council for Women was still urging the appointment of policewomen but the York Watch Committee refused. In September, the Home Office sent a letter asking police authorities to employ police women for driving, maintenance and repair of equipment, clerical, canteen and wireless work. Again, after various deputations, the Committee decided not to appoint policewomen, even though this was happening nationally. On 14th October, the Committee was asked again to consider the question of appointing policewomen. But again this did not happen. Finally in May 1942, the Home Office circular recommended women auxiliaries be appointed to take over some of the duties of policemen, especially as some were leaving to join the forces. It was agreed that 12 'auxiliary women police' be appointed. In April 1943, a leading auxiliary policewoman was appointed, but the women's salaries were still much less than their male counterparts.

Stan Wells was a taxi driver who joined the Police Reserve.

I was allocated out by the taxi people to the Royal Engineers who had an office in Wenlock Terrace. With the taxi, I was taking the engineers and officers round various camps where they had places that had gun positions. And not long after that, I joined the Reserve Police. I remember one night, there was a German aeroplane came over, and it was a brilliant moonlit night. There had been a lot of frost and snow, the roads were just like ice. This German floated round and round the city, he was dropping incendiary bombs. I was with another policeman and after he'd dropped the bombs, we were going round finding them and putting them out. That gave us an idea as to what we might be eventually getting.

I remember being on nights in the police office. There was no radio, if you wanted anybody you had to ring them. We made numerous calls to people to get them out of bed.

When they bombed Hull, we could see it ablaze. They were there two or three nights in a week, hammering it as hard as they could. We had a system where the police from different areas, had to reinforce somebody else who were under pressure due to a raid. Once I had to take a load of policemen in the car to Hull. And we'd get Leeds and Bradford men coming into York to replace them.

At Strensall camp there were thousands of troops, they were camped out all over the place. I was getting a lot of jobs convoying traffic belonging the army, through the city. All the signposts had gone. These army people didn't know their way through the city. If you had an army vehicle in front of you, you'd a little tiny glow right underneath back of the lorry on the cross member. If they were going a bit fast and it happened to stop suddenly, you could hit it. There was tanks and personnel carriers, it was really dangerous 'cos you could have got crushed. But it was a job that had to be done. I really enjoyed it 'cos I was getting out in the car instead of being inside all the time. When you were inside you were waiting for something to happen. All round the area, all the country lanes, there was like an archway of corrugated iron, about 20 feet long and about ten foot wide. They were all filled with ammunition. All down Naburn Lane there were tons and tons and tons of bombs at Common Wood and Hollicarrs Wood in Escrick.

Although extra police were employed for the duration of the war, which would indicate that more crime was expected, there is no evidence for an increase in crime in York. The court records show that the most frequent crime was the theft of bicycles. There were also cases of riding bicycles without lights, speeding and other motoring offences. Stealing and drunkenness featured quite frequently and there were many cases where soldiers were arrested for joy riding, drunken behaviour or assault. One particular incident involved a group of eight soldiers attacking a police constable. The main perpetrator got three months in prison. The only other recorded specific wartime offence was in July

1940 when a man was arrested for 'possessing ten maps which might be useful to the enemy'. He was fined £2.

THE FIRE SERVICE

In January 1938, the government asked local authorities to set up an Auxiliary Fire Service to tackle fires specifically relating to the war. There would have to be Auxiliary Fire Stations and personnel to be recruited and trained, which included experimenting with controlled fires. They were also encouraged to learn first aid. In July 1938, the Fire Brigade Act gave local authorities two years to implement this.

By late 1939, 200,000 people nationally had enrolled in the Fire Service. The Women's Auxiliary Fire Service, known as the WAFS, was formed, but the women tended to work in administrative and clerical posts, or as telephonists, drivers and dispatch riders.

In September 1940, the Fire Watchers' Order became law, making it compulsory for employees of businesses to take turns in fire watching. By the middle of 1941, York had 250 full-time auxiliary firemen.

The Fire Service in York consisted of the central HQ and two divisions, with nine auxiliary stations. The Chief Constable, Harry Herman, was the controlling officer. The stations were as follows, and tended to cover the area in which they were based –

No 1 Station. Tower Street. Five crews, and ten part-time.
No 2 Station. Fulford Tram Depot. Three crews, eight part-time.
No 3 Station. East Parade, Heworth. Four crews, 13 part-time.
No 4 Station. Football Ground, Wigginton Road. Four crews, 13 part-time.
No 5 Station. Scarcroft. Four crews, eight part-time.
No 6 Station. Forsselius Garage, Blossom Street. Three crews, seven part-time.

No 7 Station. Carriage Works, Holgate Road. Three crews, eight part-time.

No 8 Station. West Garth, Acomb. Three crews, seven part-time.

No 9 Station. Forsselius Garage, for the Tadcaster Road/Dringhouses area. Three crews, eight part-time.

When the 'stand by' message was received, an order was given out to all stations, and the men had to put on the full kit and get their gas mask, so each crew was ready. Each station had two large trailer pumps whose output was 350 gallons a minute, and varying numbers of light trailer pumps at 120 gallons a minute. There was also a fire float with a heavy pump for 800 gallons a minute, and 26 fire vehicles. Natural reserves of water were obviously used, but there were also eight steel dams erected at various points in the city, each holding 5000 gallons.

Wherever there were buildings which could be adapted for use, this was done. A toolshed with stores at Clarence Gardens, for example, was converted into an auxiliary fire station, as was a garage in Acomb in November 1939. A second hand Daimler saloon was bought for £162 to convert into a fire tender.

In November 1939, the AFS had 77 men and five women full-time, and were recruiting 60 additional firemen. In July 1940 they decided to appoint a voluntary AFS Commandant, and out of a short list, Jack Prendergast, owner of the Rialto Cinema and Ballroom, was appointed. He did not receive a salary but was given free petrol for any AFS work he did, and he was awarded the MBE for his service.

Bill Denby, born in 1906, recalls,

We had a farm in Heslington village with corn, potatoes, and sugar beet. Farm people were not allowed to go in the forces, it was a reserved occupation. They had to produce food. You had to grow certain crops and plough grass fields up.

*During the war I was a part-time fireman. Every time the siren blew
we was out on duty and we'd maybe be out seven nights in succession.
Used to stand up and I used to fall asleep at the front door. In York and
surroundings, you used to have to watch for incendiary bombs dropping on the cornfields when they got ripe, and setting them on fire.
We used to patrol the village all through the night till daylight next
morning.*

*A man lost his life on Fulford Road, they bombed there and we had to go
and help. The roof had all collapsed and bricks and supports from the
ceiling was all stood anyway. We dug so far down amongst the rubble
with our hands. You didn't know if there was anything there and you
couldn't dig with a shovel or pick or anything, because you could do
as much harm with that, After we got all the top removed, there was
a mattress from the bed, it had gone through, we knew then that was
the bedroom. We pulled some more bricks and cut some more wood up
and we'd a deep hole, the depth of a single storey. We come across a
settee upside down, and the owner of the house had been on the settee
nursing a baby, the settee had turned over and protected them. They
would have been killed otherwise. We'd loads of bricks to pull out round
about. After they'd dropped a bomb on the house it didn't explode and
knock the rubble out, it all caved into the middle where it had dropped.
We had to dig through all the rafters out of the ceiling and the bedroom
floorboards, and the mattresses.*

*Where we used to live at Heslington, we'd get all the bombers going
out from Linton, and from Elvington. On a night it was just like a
swarm of locusts going out at dusk and the racket when they used to be
coming back on a morning at dawn, you know it was really something
you never forget, hearing them go out heavily laden as though they
could hardly rise. In fact one didn't rise, it dropped in the field and blew
up. And then they used to be coming back in the morning, some with
one engine stopped. We'd stand out and watch them come in, and pray
they were all there. I never saw any German ones. You could see our lot*

*shoot a trace of bullets at something in the sky. And when they bombed
Hull we could see them drifting down, like chandeliers of light.*

Phyllis Haddacks had to firewatch and remembers one incident,

*at Park Grove School, when an undesirable character gained access by
sliding down the coal chute, undoing the door and prowling for female
firewatchers. I saw his shadow on a staircase where he was hiding. Who
said I'm not an athlete? Actually it wasn't Roger Bannister who ran
the first four minute mile, it was me. Nearby ARP officers and police
came, attracted by a window which we hadn't had time to black out.
They bellowed, "Put that light out". A scary search for the intruder
was then carried out, but by then he must have been miles away. We'd
seen him jump the wall like a frightened hare.*

*Women's Fire Service 1940, marching past Museum Gardens. Woman on right is
Evelyn Chelin. (Evelyn Chelin)*

John Waite who lived in the Hungate area, felt it was something of an adventure.

In St Saviourgate there was two shops, another little house and the Rechabite Hall, a big three storey building. We used to go up at the top of there when the war started, and sleep there once or twice a week to do your ARP fire watching. All these little fire bombs used to drop, and when a raid came, we'd go up on the roof and immediately climb over and put sand over them and put them out.

In May 1940, 150 stirrup pumps were allocated for the use of trained members of the public. In June, the Corporation decided to purchase a further 500 for resale. In May 1941, there were an additional 113 full-time auxiliary firemen taken on, totalling 250. There were also 28 full-time messengers, nine female telephonists and two female clerks. The Auxiliary Fire Service continued until May 1945.

Frank Fox was a conscientious objector and came to York in August 1941, to be an auxiliary fireman. He tells the story,

There was a staggered intake of 19 new recruits that day, and we were fitted out with uniform, steel helmet, axe and gas mask. We seemed to be a mixed bunch of conscientious objectors to military service, older men, or men not fit enough for the military. We were divided among the six sub-stations. Myself and another one or two were sent to Heworth. All the new recruits were taken daily for two weeks to Terry's factory for training, which comprised the obligatory squad drill , pump, hose-laying, and ladder drill, together with lectures on general fire-fighting. The driver was usually the pump operator. As I was able to drive, I was instructed how to operate the pumps.

Heworth sub-station was down an alley off East Parade, behind the local post office. The leading firemen were Messrs. Hodgson, Watson and Till. They were all very friendly and easy to work with. A few

men I remember on my shift were Frank Morley, Ronnie Newton, the local barber in East Parade, Bert Blanchard, Arthur Broadhead, Albert Batsleer, Paddy Walker, dispatch rider, Fred Simpson, Smith and Black. The appliances and watch-room were housed in what had been a garage. To one side of the exercise yard was a prefabricated building housing the dormitory, canteen-cum-restroom, and the officers' room. Syd Watson told me that Mrs. Rennison across from his house wanted another lodger, and as her husband was unfortunately incarcerated in a hospital at Acomb, she was glad of the extra income. Her son-in-law, Chris Frame, was a regular fireman, the other lodger worked at Barr & Stroud. We helped around the house and garden, decorating as and when necessary.

The Auxiliary Fire Service, Heworth sub station. Billy Barker is in front of sandbags (second row); two to his left is Paddy Walker, dispatch rider. In front of Billy is Arthur Broadhead who died in the York Baedeker Raid. Far right on same row is Frank Morley. Mr Day, the station officer in charge, is seated in centre. To his left is Leading Fireman Percy Till; on far right is Mrs Hill, part-time watch room telephonist. (Frank Fox)

On my first free Sunday I went to the Monkgate Methodist Church service. After the service I was approached by Mr. J.R. Fearnley, whose son was also in the A.F.S., who took me under his wing throughout the whole of my service in York. He helped me through when times became tough. Other church members also befriended me and offered hospitality, in spite of food rationing. I was welcomed into the church life and became a member of the well-known church choir.

At Heworth we had a system of alarm bells. One ring indicated that the officer in charge was required in the watch-room. Two rings meant an alert for enemy activity in the North East. Three rings indicated a full alert, and 'Action Stations'. At first we worked two weeks on days and two weeks on nights, changing over at 6 a.m. and 6 p.m. We had a day off every eight days. When it fell on a Saturday we had Sunday off as well. On starting a shift the first duty was to check the contents of each pump. We worked during the day keeping the station and appliances clean and having various drills.

There was an 'invasion' exercise on November 4th, 1941, when York was 'captured'. Instruction was sometimes given during the evening between 7 and 9, when the part-time firemen came in, and lady watch-room part-time operators took over. We were instructed on the many activities likely to be met with when duty called, and told of the experiences from those towns which had been targeted by the Luftwaffe, including the type of bombs being used. We were asked to look out for anti-personnel bombs, or butterfly bombs as they were called, due to the small propellers attached, to allow them to drop without exploding on impact. During the day and after midnight the watch-room was manned by the full-time men. One day we were taken to the Central Fire Station and given an idea of the duties of regular firemen, how to ascend the turn-table ladder and the importance of attaching the safety belt to the correct rung.

At Heworth we had three trailer pumps, a Coventry Climax, a Harland and a Sigmund. As towing vehicles we had a second-hand Packard, another old saloon and Mr. Boag's coal lorry, which he parked in our yard. On September 23rd, 1941, we received a new Austin truck with seats down each side, under which we could keep additional equipment. York was very fortunate in having the Ouse and its tributaries for a back-up water supply in case the hydrants dried up. One of the first jobs we did at Heworth was to collect cinders from local boiler houses. We didn't have a JCB to load and unload the lorry! It was more physical than most of us had been used to, but we tackled the job with gusto. We made a cinder path down a grassy slope to a small stream in Heworth in the Tang Hall Lane area, so that the small Sigmund pump could be manhandled down to the water, if and when required.

Free time was available for table tennis, darts and draughts. We had inter-station matches. All the time we prepared, trained and waited for action. From time to time we had emergency drills when we would get three rings, and had to assemble our pumps at the end of Tang Hall Lane as a possible reinforcement column wherever required.

On one occasion at Heworth we were drying wet hose on the roof of the dormitory. I went over the ridge and too near the chimney from the boiler beneath, and fell through the asbestos, which unknown to me was brittle at that point where the boiler chimney came through, landing on my feet in the dormitory. L/F Watson watching from the yard, thought I had fallen off the back of the building, but when he went round I wasn't there, of course.

Albert [Batsleer], who after the war became a vicar, and subsequently a Canon, had quite a lively wit. One man on his day off drove a sugar lorry for a chocolate factory, and when he complained about having some sugar irritating his eye, Albert suggested he cried in his tea, sugar being on ration. It was decided by the powers that be, that at dusk a man from Heworth should be sent to the top of the static gasholder, which dominated the skyline for miles around the city. There was no gas in the gasholder since apparently it may have exploded if hit by a bomb, or shrapnel. We accessed the curved top by climbing up the zig-zag open staircase on the outside. There was a round hut in the centre at the top containing chairs and a table and a Rediffusion radio. We were on four hour shifts up there, modified accordingly during the summer nights, and there was also an Observer Corps man with us. One company officer asked Albert and myself, as we had been at school more recently than most men there, whether it would be possible to pin-point fires from two different vantage points in the city. We answered, "One fire probably but several fires would be almost impossible". In any case special instrumentation would have been required to pin-point the fires. Many people had Rediffusion in their homes, and there was one at Heworth sub-station. We got all the popular tunes of the day, ad nauseam.

I was fortunate in being a driver as I was well occupied in various driving duties, collecting cars from Bridlington, taking men to various locations. Some of the men had previously been sent to assist the Liverpool Fire Service before I joined. Actual service under air raid conditions had not been experienced, so we did not know what situation we might have to meet. We waited in anticipation. Relaxation was provided by football matches against other divisions and service teams. We managed to beat the police fairly easily on one occasion, but the armed forces teams had physical training instructors and ex-professional footballers in their ranks, and were a different proposition.

On April 29th, 1942, [the night of the York Baedeker Raid] *at around 2.35 a.m., we were asleep in the dormitory, when the bell sounded. Three rings indicating 'action stations'. I thought, "'Oh, not another reinforcement exercise". Hurriedly preparing for duty with gas mask and helmet, I went to the door. On opening it, there in the sky above, facing, was the beautiful but chilling sight of a parachute flare. This was to be no exercise! It transpired that the German planes had been*

45

flying north up the east coast, presumably going to a coastal port. When they approached Flamborough Head they had unexpectedly turned west, and made for York. It transpired that the first Pathfinders had dropped incendiaries to mark out the target area, although we were unaware at the time. Fred Simpson, who had longer service than myself, elected to be driver, and therefore, pump operator. A very significant decision it turned out to be. Mr. Black, a part-time leading fireman ,was in charge, and Arthur Broadhead and myself were the other two crew members. As we went down East Parade we dropped all the available windows to save ourselves being cut by flying glass should we be near enough to a bomb explosion. We were fired up by adrenaline and excited at the prospect of action at last, but had no idea what we should be faced with.

At Wigginton Road, we were immediately sent to the Bootham area where house fires had been reported. We went over the bridge near Rowntree's and down the side of the railway. Over the railway fence a Bofors gun was hopefully firing tracer shells into the night sky. We manhandled the pump into Bootham Crescent, where a house roof was ablaze on the opposite side. We located a hydrant and the hose was connected. Arthur tucked the branch pipe into his belt and ran out the first length of hose diagonally across the street, and I ran out the second length. I asked Arthur to go back and check the connection. I signalled to Fred to open the valve. We were too engrossed to notice what might have been going on above us. I saw Arthur walk back to check the coupling as I requested, and watched the hose filling with water, when a bomb dropped at the edge of the road directly opposite the pump and about 10 yards from where I was standing. I found myself on the floor, my head towards the bomb. The noise was terrific, the loudest noise I had ever heard. It seemed to go on a long time. Unknown to me at the time other bombs had dropped further down the street. I covered my neck with my hands for safety and bits and pieces were flying around. I had a bang on my helmet and discovered later it was dented and impregnated with brick dust. I have no doubt it had saved my life. An old man was groaning near me, perhaps a fire watcher. I got him to his feet and took him to his house nearby. The front door was off its hinges and at a crazy angle. I went to see the man next day and he seemed to be all right, except for a cut hand.

The pump was ablaze and when I got back the leading fireman was speaking to Fred, who was sitting on the garden wall. I did not realise then that Fred had been injured. I was in a state of shock and concussed. Realising the pump was out of action, I suggested to Mr. Black that I should go back to Wigginton Road for a replacement pump to which he agreed. The concussion had left me quite unconcerned and fearless as I drove back. I only saw part-time Station Officer Davies at Wigginton Road, but he said I must stay at the station. All his pumps may have been out already. It must have been obvious to him that I was in a bit of a state, dishevelled, with a dented helmet. He noticed a tear in my right legging which had been done by a piece of shrapnel, causing a slight wound on my thigh. He insisted an applying a plaster. The piece of shrapnel was found in my wellington when I took it off later that day. I still have it. When the 'all clear' sounded and day began to break, I ferried water from the River Foss to the static water tank in the football ground car park. I made several trips. On the grapevine we understood afterwards that it was secretly known that York was to be the target that night, but the German code had only just been broken, and they may have suspected if they had been met with a vigorous response on arrival.

In all the confusion I had not seen Arthur Broadhead at the scene in Bootham Crescent and was told later that he had been blown to bits by the bomb. He had been walking back to the coupling as I had requested and must have been much nearer the bomb than I was. I have always had the feeling that I should have checked the coupling myself, as I had made it, and would have suffered the same fate instead. Fred Simpson had been badly injured and admitted to hospital. He had suffered shrapnel wounds to his face. His jaws and one eye had been damaged.

He was in hospital for several weeks. He had his jaws reconstructed and an eye taken out. He had decided to drive, when I could so easily have been told to. I suffered from concussion for several weeks afterwards and behaved somewhat like a zombie, going through the motions. When I touched the left side of my head I had no feeling there for a few weeks. I went to Arthur's funeral on May 4th.

After the war I lived over on the west coast and in 1991 I was motivated to find Arthur's grave. It was not maintained and had no decent headstone. I resolved to supply one as I believed it should have a suitable inscription. This was done as follows, "F/M Arthur Broadhead. Killed in Action. Bootham Terrace. April 29th. 1942. R.I.P."

Frank Fox at the grave of Arthur Broadhead, 1991 (Frank Fox)

Once I had recovered from concussion I was subsequently filled with apprehension whenever the sirens sounded, but I was determined not to give way in face of danger. My faith kept me going and I would recite a verse to myself from a hymn as follows:

> *'Faint not Christian, will ye yield?*
> *Will ye quit the fateful field?*
> *Will ye flee in danger's hour?*
> *Know ye not your Saviour's power?'*

In hindsight I was almost glad that I had nearly lost my life on that fateful night and the subsequent fear. I could not be accused of being cowardly.

Home Guard parade past Mansion House 1944 (Maurice Bowling)

THE HOME GUARD

When the government appealed for men to join the Local Defence Volunteers, 250,000 signed up within 24 hours. The first mounted squadron of the LDV in the country was at Bulmer, covering the York to Easingwold area. The name was changed to the Home Guard in 1940, and by 1943 it comprised 1.8 million men. During the war 1,600 were killed on duty. They were stood down in December 1944.

Our knowledge of the Home Guard comes mostly from the TV comedy series *'Dad's Army'*. In reality the role was far more serious with members as committed to serving their country as the armed forces. John Birch was one of them.

I thought I might as well go in the Home Guard. We used to have exercises with the regular army. I know we had one where they gave me a label and I was supposed to be a casualty. They come and took me to Haxby and then to crown all, when it had all finished, they took me back to Clifton and dropped me there. Then I had to walk home from there to Heworth.

Bob Ferguson 2005 (Van Wilson)

Les Benson recalls,

I remember the Home Guard drilling at the bottom of Marygate in civvy clothes with armbands on and a load of sticks. They called them the LDV Brigade; 'Look, duck and vanish'.

Cooke, Troughton & Sims Home Guard platoon 1942 (Bob Ferguson)

Bob Ferguson came to York in the 1930s, and worked at Cooke, Troughton and Sims. The company had its own Home Guard unit.

We were transferred up to Haxby Road where another factory was built to accommodate us. During the war we had to transfer our production over from optical equipment like microscopes for survey work to tank periscopes and equipment that was useful to the war effort. We got involved in the Home Guard. While we were working, we had periods of time training. We had a couple of hours marching outside the factory and at weekends we used to go to another part of the city working in cooperation with other companies.

When we really started, we just had the LDV badges on, and then First World War equipment like Ross and Remington rifles. At week-ends we used to go out to Strensall and there we took part on the rifle ranges firing targets and throwing HE 36 grenades. Gradually things became more efficient in the Home Guard. Early on we had our issue of uniforms, but some of these were ill fitting and we had to get our wives to alter them to fit us. It all stemmed from the period when they were evacuating Dunkirk, they were expecting the Germans to come over to this country. Fortunately it didn't work out that way.

In June 1940, after Dunkirk, newspapers carried advice on what to do if the country was invaded. This included not to give any German anything, to hide all food and bicycles, to check any orders with the official source, the local ARP or policeman. And above all to keep watch for anyone acting suspiciously.

Jack Smith was also involved.

I was in a reserved occupation on the farm. I passed all me exams for Home Guard, map reading, rifle shooting and machine guns, and spigot motors, and I got all me certificates.

We had a meeting about three times a week and we had to be on Home Guard on a Sunday as well, then we had church parade once a month. You always used to have mock battles, one platoon against another. I loved it.

The whole group used to go to the searchlight unit once a fortnight, take turns, you'd stay there all night and if they had a warning, you had to go and wake the area Home Guard. And it only came about once a fortnight, then you get a rest, 'cos you were working every day as well.

Peter Goater was unable to go into the forces because

I was in a reserved occupation. So I joined the Home Guard. I was in the power station platoon on Foss Islands Road, It was a mass of turbines. You could see it across the cooling tower. I was there the night after the Baedeker Raid and some more planes came. When you're in khaki you've got gaiters on and you've got turndowns over your gaiters. I was going across the corporation yard, 'cos I was on the telephone exchange which was internal, and as I crossed the yard, this incendiary bomb dropped about two yards away and before it goes boom, it spit and it spit and it burnt the turndown, with it not being near my leg. I was all right really. I just knocked it out. There were some bombs that didn't go off, they dropped one of those right on the roof of the power station, it went right in between the turret, it hit a turbine. All the factories rung in, 'cos all their lights had gone. "What's happened to the power station?" Terry's rung first, then the firm I worked for, Cooke's, then Rowntree's rung. "What's happening to our lighting system?" But it came back. The next day after the raid, I was on duty in Coney Street. All the windows were out and there was jewellery all over the place. Two of us, we'd a rifle each to stop looters, I hate to tell you who the looters were, they were specials, [special constables]. At that time we had the Wellington Inn, down Alma Terrace, and a chap came in and he says to my mother, "How would you like to buy these watch straps?" It was a paradise for looters was Coney Street.

Home Guard standing down, Knavesmire 1944. Bob Ferguson is on right hand line, 8th from front. (Bob Ferguson)

Looting after air raids was taken so seriously that it was an offence punishable by death. Although people mention cases of looting, there were no convictions listed in the court records.

Peter continues,

In the Home Guard, we were just like soldiers, we had proper uniform. You had rifle drill, and we went over the Black Watch assault course at Strensall. Strensall then was common land, it used to be full of sheep and if you threw one, [a grenade], it didn't kill any sheep but the shrapnel got into them and they ran off like mad.

53

The actual Home Guard purpose was because we knew the area, the Germans wouldn't. When we left the Wellington, we went to live at the Tiger at Haxby. I transferred to the Home Guard at Haxby. You had farmer's sons which knew all the area, knew exactly where to go, it was a self-defence for the country.

Maureen Jerrum's father was in the Home Guard.

They used to parade at night time. When the aircraft siren sounded, they had to go to a point, north, south, east and so forth. When he was released from the Home Guard, he used to put his fireman's clothes on and go to York to help if a fire wanted putting out. He used to come home, get dressed and go to work at the railway. He had three jobs. We had a German parachute come down in the back of our garden and my father dragged the pilot out and carried him up to Strensall camp. They had an ambulance, but he'd lost an arm.

THE WOMEN'S VOLUNTARY SERVICE

The WVS, as it was known, was very active during the war. The members ran rest centres, mobile canteens and clothing stores for people to swap garments. They gave talks on nutrition and how to Make Do and Mend with clothing, trained in first aid and sometimes fire duties, organised war nurseries, helped people after raids by finding accommodation and tracing the missing and wounded, and they also gave support to lonely old people who found it hard to cope with the war.

They also sent parcels abroad. The village of Cawood near York, for example, made parcels containing 'comforts and other articles' to be sent to the men of Cawood overseas. Each parcel contained socks, two pencils, biscuits, cake, cigarettes, two chocolates, writing pad, shaving soap, three hankies, boiled sweets, liquorice allsorts, foot powder, Vaseline, playing cards and cheese!

The Grange at Cawood held knitting and sewing parties. From October 1939 to October 1940, 3,791 knitted garments were sent to Lady Ramsden's Central Hospital Supply Service, for distribution to the forces. In April 1940, the York WVS sent 1000 woollen articles for the crew of HMS *York*, and 1000 items for the Royal Navy and the RAF. They also provided some knitted helmets, mittens, dressing gowns and pillow cases and nightshirts for the Red Cross. In May 1940, the Bugthorpe (another local village) knitting party sent three jerseys, four vests, two spencers (a kind of over vest), two pairs of socks, two pixie bonnets and two scarves to Polish refugees. They then produced sixteen scarves, 17 pairs of socks, nine helmets, ten pairs of mittens, two pairs of gloves, three pullovers and four pairs of wristlets for local men in the forces. They also sent chocolates and cigarettes.

Sheila White was 14 when the war broke out and went to work full-time at Rowntree's. She also spent her spare time doing voluntary work.

We worked from 7.30 on a morning to 5.30, and Saturday morning till 12. But my friend and I also went to Naburn Hospital. That was voluntary, on a Tuesday and Thursday night. There were two wards for the soldiers, only broken arms and things like that, nothing drastic. We'd write letters for them if their arms were in slings, take the water round and give them a shave. We used to go to the Red Cross at Rowntree's too.

One of the big activities run by the WVS was the Station Canteen. At the end of the war the helpers, like Joyce Elliott, were presented with a certificate.

I used to go two or three nights a week. When the troop trains came in, the sailors were always first off 'cos they could jump off and run.

Joyce Elliott 2005 (Brian Freeborn)

We had some trains that they couldn't get off. They were going to the front. They came from Scotland and were going down to the ports. I never charged the lads who were going to war. They had the doors locked. We used to shove tea and food through.

Tea and sandwiches were known as 'char and wads'. Mrs Brooke also helped out.

The Station Canteen had a reputation all over the country. We had eight to ten on each shift. We used to take big trolleys and urns down the lift and under and out to the No 8 platform. Out the lads would rush when trains got in. They brought their own pots but we supplied them as well. It was hectic for about ten minutes. They were really longing for this cup of tea. The other shift was half ten or eleven. They set two girls making sandwiches, spam, tomatoes and lettuce in different layers, it was quite scrumptious.

WVS Canteen at York Station during World War Two. (York Oral History Society)

York Station Canteen invitation, 1946, to Mrs May Potter. (Van Wilson)

As the 'fighting men' who passed through the station were provided with free refreshments, there were appeals to the public to help finance this, and a lot of people gave donations.

Phyllis Haddacks, as well as teaching full-time and taking turns at occasional firewatching, also worked in the hospital, helping the nurses and cooking meals. And she had another task.

> *We used to do a lot of voluntary work in the war. One of them was helping to make camouflage nets and they used to lay them out in front of the Art Gallery, and sew them because there was plenty of space to do it there.*

Salvage collecting (what would now be called recycling) became compulsory. The WVS were involved, and children as well as adults were encouraged, through school and such groups as the Boy Scouts, to recycle paper, cardboard, pots and aluminium for aeroplanes and vehicles, hot water bottles and hoses to make inflatable boats. All food scraps were collected by corporation wagons and put into dustbins for feeding pigs. Waste was to be utilized, as the City Engineer, Charles Minter, explains.

> *We started up a system of collecting kitchen waste from houses and took it down to our yard and put it in three digesters and cooked this stuff up to make it safe to serve to animals. We sold it to pig dealers and anybody else. We also collected waste paper and baled that and sold it, and collected tins and sold them. We did a lot of good work that way.*

Like other towns and cities in England, York ran various fundraising initiatives such as Wings for Victory, Warship Week, Build a Spitfire and Salute the Soldier week. These were good for boosting morale and making ordinary people aware that they could do something to help the bigger picture. In this way thousands were raised to build ships and new aircraft. In one of his famous speeches, in June 1940, Churchill said,

> *We have today a very large and powerful military force, 1,250,000 men plus 500,000 defence volunteers.*

It is an acknowledged fact that the war was won not just by the soldiers, sailors and air force, but by the ordinary people using all their spare time in helping the war effort, doing what they could for their country.

CHAPTER FOUR

THE WOMEN'S LAND ARMY

The Women's Land Army (colloquially known as the Cinderellas of the Soil) was originally formed during the First World War, and reformed in summer 1939. At that stage it was clear that food would have to be rationed, and that land would be required for agriculture. Over 1000 women volunteered in that early period. By 1941 this figure had risen to 20,000, and by 1944 the number had increased to 80,000. Although farmers were deemed to be in a reserved occupation, farm workers and labourers were not, and these men were conscripted. This meant that women were necessary to fill their roles, and therefore became vital in the production of food for the nation.

Women's Land Army recruitment poster

To begin with, farmers were reluctant to allow young women to help on the farm. Some labourers did not get called up straightaway which meant that some of the women who volunteered for the WLA got sent home as superfluous, or were used as domestic workers. The wages of the WLA were set by the Agricultural Wages Board, and over 18s

Women's Land Army – harrowing near York (York Oral History Society)

should have got £1.12s a week. This was for 50 hours in summer, and 48 in winter, with Saturday afternoon and Sunday off. This did not always happen, and some farmers overcharged for food and lodgings. At harvest time, Land Army girls would work far more than 50 hours. Like evacuees, the women experienced both hostility and hospitality. Some women were treated as one of the family by the farmers they worked for, and others were misused and exploited, and suffered real loneliness and homesickness. The first contingent of recruits to the WLA in Yorkshire reported on 20th October 1939.

Lilian Faulkner worked on a farm in the war.

I had a land army job. We used to help with stookies, with cheese, and hay, and topping carrots. I supervised a few gangs of schoolchildren picking potatoes. Now they have these big combines, but then they had a horse that went round with a spinner, spun the potatoes out and the children would pick them up and put them in buckets. It used to be great fun, then going back to the farmhouse for tea.

Doreen Angus was 16 when war broke out. She lists the choices available to women.

> *When I registered it was nursing, munitions or the Land Army they were recruiting for at that period. And I chose the Land Army.*

Many women who joined the WLA went to live in hostels, which were in large houses requisitioned in the vicinity of the farms, and were sent out in twos and threes to their work. Others actually lived in the farmhouse with the family, and this often took some getting used to.

Doreen Angus as young woman (Doreen Angus)

Doreen Angus 2005 (Van Wilson)

The WLA brought together women of all backgrounds and classes, so adjustment was needed. Some women were given training before the work started, but not all. Doreen was thrown in at the deep end.

I didn't get any training. I went for a medical first, to a lady doctor on the Mount. And then the farmer had asked for two land girls and we went straight on to the farm, another girl and I. It was a dairy farm and when we went he said, "You can start on Dolly, she's quiet"! It took a long time for the milk to come! We didn't really have much idea, but we were billeted with the cowman which was next to the farmhouse, and he explained. But then the other land girl wasn't very happy being on a farm and she wanted a transfer. I think she liked the work, but she wanted more company, so I was left on my own. And I worked there right until almost the end of the war.

When I got used to the farm work I liked it and I didn't mind being on my own. We had good food and that was something, and plenty of milk. The farmer's wife where I stayed, she was very good. When I was a girl at home I didn't like rice pudding, but we had a lot of rice pudding there, but it was creamy and lovely. Bacon was home-cured which was fatty, but you were hungry so you got used to it.

It was a dairy farm, it was milking every day. They provided the uniform, an aertex shirt, a green jumper, jodhpurs, long socks and shoes. I think we were given wellington boots. We wore overalls normally [for milking], but then on a Saturday we used to get back in our cords and our breeches and as soon as we finished milking, we were able to cycle into York for the evening. We milked very carefully because if you missed, the milk got hard on the cords. When we'd finished and the cows were turned out, then we had to make sure the cowshed was clean. We used to stand at the end with a big shovel, and if we saw the cow pop its tail up we used to run with the shovel so it wouldn't make a mess! Happy times.

It would be about 6 o'clock start and in the winter time it was picking turnips, and we used to have to pick them and top and tail them. There was no machines then. And sugar beet we had to pull, and potatoes. The cowman and the lad, they'd go along hoeing, and I used to have to follow and pick the bits up.

I remember it was a really cold frosty morning and we were topping and tailing and throwing them in a pile on the side and going along the line. And I missed and chopped [part of] my thumb off with the thing, and we were two fields away from the farm. I thought I must hold my arm up to stop the blood and it happened to be running all over, and the farmer was milking. I ran in the cowshed and I said, "I've cut me thumb". He looked round and he said, "I thought you'd cut your blooming head, the noise you're making". Anyway, the silly man put cotton wool on it, so that night I had to ride into York to get it dressed. The nurse had to pick all the cotton wool off and she dressed it and I came back and the next morning it was a bit sore but he said, "It won't hurt you to milk".

I also took one of the horses to Appleton Roebuck to be shod. It was the old farm horse and no saddle and you had to sit on that and it was practically a day's job because you plodded all the way. It was quite pleasant really, apart from the fact that there was Italian prisoners of war along the road there, and they'd come to the fence and make silly remarks. I used to take me sandwiches and something to drink and then plod all the way back.

Doreen had never ridden a horse before and never driven a tractor. But she was still expected to do so!

The first time I went with a tractor, the farmer was driving and he was ploughing, and it was a lovely day and he said, "Watch what I'm doing", and I was watching while I was standing up behind him and it was lovely! And then he said, "You can just finish that field", and that

Land Army girls march through York

was it! But that's when a bit of trouble started, because you're driving the tractor, and pulling the plough when you get to the end to turn, and I was doing not too bad at first and was getting quite proud of myself, but then I missed the turning and the thing went in the ditch. I had to leave it because it had stopped, and come back all the way to the farm and I was scared to have to tell him. He wasn't very pleased, I was more nervous then than I had been when I started.

So there was tractoring, horses, and threshing. The threshing machine would come, and then it would go to another farm another day and we would go and help. It was always, "My girl will carry the chaff", which was the dirtiest job. There weren't combine harvesters like they have now. There'd be one man throwing it up on to the machine, another man going through the machine, the man at the end catching the corn or wheat, and all the muck that came from the thing, like the chaff or the hairy bits off the barley, you slung it on your back and tipped it and then started again.

When Vera and I were there, one of the cows had calved in a field and he sent us with a barrow to bring it back. He said, "If it's a heifer bring it back or if it's a bull calf, leave it and we'll get it later". Well we got there to see this poor little calfling and we hadn't a clue what it was, it had its legs up in the air and we're looking and, "No I can't see what it could be". So we just slung it in this barrow and took it back! Hoped it was the right sex when we got there!

I remember my father coming out one day to see me on his bike and we'd been threshing and it was barley, and the long hairs would get everywhere, they'd get under your eyelids and you'd have sore eyes. He said, "You've been crying, haven't you?" And I said, "No I haven't, we've been threshing". He said, "Because if you're crying your mother said you have to come home".

When it was haytime and it was a moon, we worked while it was light, getting all the hay in. Often after tea, if we'd been harvesting, we'd do stooks then. We'd have to put the sheaves up into little stooks and leave them to dry. We did have evenings out and it was nice. We'd come into York on our bicycles quite often and go to the De Grey Rooms, dancing in our hobnail shoes. There was some village lads which weren't bad. We'd often go for a bike ride with them. Or then we met an airman, perhaps. There was an air field at Acaster, and once or twice we went there to a bit of a social do. If we'd decided to go on the bus, we'd cycle to Bishopthorpe and leave the bicycles at a farm and get the bus to York. We were paid about 19 shillings, but then he had to claim so much for our keep out of that, so we had very little money.

If we were just doing a normal day's work like being in the fields or milking, we'd perhaps see if there was anything happening in the village. But if like at haytime when it was fine weather and you had to get the hay in, you'd just keep on working until the last load had gone and it was dark.

65

We were hedging one day, Philip, the cowman, and I, and it was really wet and nasty. The cowman put a sacking on my shoulders to keep me dry. The farmer didn't seem to realise we were getting very wet. But then we got another job which I used to hate and I would've given up then. He used to get the cows in and we used to have to clean them. They'd been sitting in muck and you had to scrape it off their backs. I know we were kept dry in the cow shed, but it wasn't very pleasant. You scraped it off as fast as you could, and then cleaned it out. We had to hose the cow shed down, and the dairy. We used to have to clean all the dairy things 'cos the milk went through big coolers, it was then put into churns and taken down to the gate and it was picked up like that. We didn't have a bull, but when the cows needed servicing we'd have a bull from another farm. We cleaned the pigs too, and hens. Hens I didn't like, the hen house was messy, and fleas I think in there. I got jaundice while I was there and I cycled into York to see the doctor. And I'm quite sure it was getting soaking wet that did it. My back was absolutely wringing wet with the rain. I had to stay at home, I think it was a fortnight. That was the only time I was ill. Every so often we did get a Saturday off. When Vera went and I was on my own it was more difficult.

Sometimes it seems ages and ages ago, and then other times something happens, like when I saw the film [The Land Girls], and all sorts came back then. Some of it was realistic, except we didn't have a nice young man come in to see us at night!

The WLA continued, as did rationing, into the 1950s. The Land Army alone received no post-gratuity.

Doreen was one of the women responsible for campaigning for a memorial to the women in the Second World War, as was Mildred Veal, who also appears in this volume. The campaign was begun in York by Major David Robertson and funds were raised with large donations, such as the £800,000 raised by Betty Boothroyd who appeared on 'Who

Land Army girls, Yorkshire

Wants to Be a Millionaire?' to raise money for the cause and many, many smaller donations, (my own small donation being in memory of my mother who served in the ATS during the war). The campaign was successful and the memorial was finally unveiled by the Queen in July 2005, after seven years of campaigning, and sixty years after the end of the war! The Land Army were only officially allowed to march a few years ago. Doreen continues,

I heard someone on the radio and she said she didn't think the Land Army should be on the memorial because she was a farmer's daughter and she didn't get any medals. Well we didn't get any medals. We didn't get anything at all.

She probably was working on a farm, but it would be quite different. She could say, "I don't feel like getting up this morning", and that would be it. And now there's machines for lifting potatoes, machines for lifting beetroot. We had to pick it, knock it together, and lay it in lines for it to be collected.

But it was always pushed aside somehow, the Land Army, I don't know why, perhaps they didn't think we were in any danger, but some of the land girls that were down south, they used to have all the planes going over. They had to run and hide and keep out of the way of the bombs. This memorial, it's for all women. I know the servicewomen worked hard and they were away from home, but there were other women who drove buses and trains, and then there were women who had to stay at home and look after the children, and took families in, and evacuees. On the memorial there's all the uniforms hanging up, you can see which is the Land Army. We've got that funny pork pie hat!

In January 2008, the Environment Secretary, Hilary Benn, announced that all surviving members of the WLA would receive a commemorative badge in recognition of their service during the war. Members had been campaigning for several decades so this was a very welcome announcement.

Letter of appreciation to Doreen Angus for service in WLA. (Doreen Angus)

CHAPTER FIVE

RATIONS AND FASHIONS

Salvage Your Cardboard poster

Don't Waste Food poster

As early as August 1939, stores were urging their customers to stock up in case of impending war. S. Border, a grocer in Coney Street, for example, suggested buying a number of items 'for your store cupboard'. These included tins of brisket beef, tongue, and baked beans, galantines of chicken and ham, tea, jam and tinned milk, as well as tinned apricots, pears and peaches. There was a surfeit of plums that summer and so people were urged to make plum jam and can it. Rationing did not actually begin in the UK until January 1940. Ships carrying goods from abroad were regularly torpedoed by German U-boats so supplies became very short. The first items to be rationed were butter or lard to four ounces a week, sugar to twelve ounces, and bacon or ham to four ounces, though these amounts were decreased later on. Meat rationing started in March, and this was measured by cost rather than weight. Each person was allowed meat to the value of 1s 2d (about 6p today). By July, tea, cooking fat, margarine and cheese were added, and by March 1941, treacle, marmalade and jam joined the list. Although certain items were not officially rationed, they could still be in short supply. Eggs were limited to one per person per week, and in 1942 dried egg powder came in, which was used instead of real eggs.

Your Children's Food in Wartime pamphlet

In October 1939, the Women's Voluntary Service appealed for 100 women helpers to assist at the public library in issuing the ration books. Each person in the country was issued with a buff coloured ration book, and tokens were torn out and given to the shopkeeper. Most people had to register with a particular grocer. Occasionally if a grocer got stocks of some luxury item, they would advertise the fact, and once word got out, queues would form until all the stocks were sold. Pregnant women and small children were issued with extra tokens, and parents were encouraged to buy cod liver oil and orange juice for young children, to ensure they got vital vitamins. It was also quite usual for people to swap goods. If someone was not fond of tea, for instance, they might swap their ration of tea for sugar or butter. Of course the system was open to corruption, and a 'black market' developed, where people would obtain goods illegally and then sell them on.

Strangely enough, bread was never actually rationed until after the war, but supplies had to be eked out, and loaves were made from home-grown oatmeal instead of wheatmeal, which apparently did not taste as good.

Dig for Victory poster

The Dig for Victory campaign began early in 1940, and people were encouraged to use whatever garden they had to grow fruit and vegetables. Additionally open land and parks were requisitioned for growing produce, and farmers had to plough up their meadowland. In York, parks were dug up, and the Eye of York, the open space outside the Castle Museum, was covered in allotments, which were still there for the Royal Visit in 1948. Families were also urged to buy their own pig or chickens, so that they could provide meat and eggs.

Alwyn Banks recalls promoting the campaign.

I became an apprentice electrician with York Corporation in 1943. I was the showroom boy and one of the first jobs I had was to convert the showroom windows into a farmyard where we had live rabbits and chickens and signs for Dig for Victory.

Bill and Nora Denby lived on a farm in Heslington. Bill recalls having to live on rations.

We had to eat less, there was no bran or anything, what we call whole-meal flour. The flour was very dark and didn't cook very well but we made do with it. It's surprising what you can learn to do if you've got to. We all had the same, there was no surplus. In those days you'd eat practically anything. That was when spam first came, from America. We used to think that was gorgeous. We wouldn't buy it now! I think I ate more jam, there was plenty of jam in wartime to last me the rest of my days.

Bill Denby, 1930s
(York Oral History Society)

This was because Nora was very resourceful.

I used to bottle fruit and you can do that without sugar. I think you could get saccharine to sweeten things. But I'm sure we were all healthier then than we are now. At least we weren't fat. Beef and all meats was rationed. It was nearly all lamb in those days. Lamb, lamb, lamb, we got sick of it.

We kept our own chickens. We had about a dozen hens and they used to lay. When they got old we used to get some fresh ones and put them in the pot. And I think country people are better at being thrifty than townfolk, even today. When I see some of the things they throw away now, I could make another meal out of it!

You had to tighten your belts, but we always had plenty of potatoes and vegetables growing on the farm. Apples we grew on our own trees, and local stalls in the market had seasonal fruit like gooseberries, raspberries and things grown in this country.

They used to come and count your pigs. If one died you had to have a very lengthy report on why it had died and where it had gone. A lot of folks used to cheat, have a few pigs that they hadn't declared and sell them on the black market. We knew a few farmers that were on that.

Geoffrey Iredale, as a boy, helped his farmer friend, but it was not always straightforward.

The sun shone from a clear blue sky on that day in August 1944. Working with my friend Bob, the farmer, in the cornfields of his Slingsby farm to harvest the barley, good progress was being made when the binder decided it had had enough. A small part had broke, requiring a replacement from an agricultural machine company in York, a return journey of 40 miles. This provoked a curse from Bob, realising that no more cutting of barley was going to be possible that day, and would the good weather hold up for another few days?

We set off in the old bullnosed Morris. The trip went well until we reached Strensall. Here the military had set up two half barriers in the road (a chicane in today's terminology). Every vehicle passing through was stopped for a check of identity cards. I had set out without mine so was taken to the guard room. While doing farm work I constantly used my old football jersey from school days. This had horizontal bands of brown and yellow, colours apparently very close to the Italian prisoner of war uniforms. This was unknown to me, of course. We were detained for two hours whilst phone calls were made to Slingsby to prove our identity. The delay caused more problems for Bob, who was very unhappy at the hold-up, wondering if the farm machinery company would be closed when we reached York. After release we drove to York as fast as the old Morris would go, got the part and headed home. Over the next few days the harvest was gathered, and stacked in the yard, ready for eventual threshing. I wore that jersey until it was threadbare, but with no more problems.

Avril Appleton remembers

taking the ration books to the shop in Heworth. We weren't so bad because we lived on the Stray, and we had big gardens at the backs. And my dad used to grow tomatoes and vegetables. We kept chickens, geese and ducks. I had the job of getting the eggs. Sometimes we used to get rats and once there was this dead rat and they made me get it out. We always had fresh chickens, and my mother was cooking these chickens and there was always this horrible smell in the house. You killed the chickens and then they flapped for a bit.

My mother got these rabbits that were called Flemish Giants because she'd have it for the meat and she'd make clothes from the fur. They were awful, great big things, couldn't make a pet of them. And when

*they did get killed and mother sent the fur away, it cost her no end
getting it cleaned and all it made was a small pair of mitts for me,
which I promptly lost. My father was always taking eggs to people.
They used to say, "Can I have half a dozen eggs?", for somebody's little
girl who was ill or something. I think he would barter the eggs for some
meat or sausages. They used to preserve them in this water glass so
they would keep fresh for quite a while.* [Fridges were not common-
place before the 1950s]. *Tomatoes were bottled so we always had fried
tomatoes and a bit of bacon, eggs, and bread and dripping. And also she
bottled onions and red cabbage. She was always bottling and making
chutney and jam. We had to go and pick rosehips and made it into
rosehip syrup.*

*There was a big shortage of meat. I remember once my mother came
home and she'd got some horsemeat. We said, "Oh good", 'cos we
thought we'd got something different. Horrible it was, couldn't eat it, it
was really coarse and tough. My uncle was in India so my auntie came
to live with us with her two children. Once we pinched this dried fruit,
me and my brother and my cousin. It was such a carry on, we were all
interviewed separately to try to find out who'd eaten this dried fruit. It
was a terrible sin. But I don't remember going hungry. My job was to
go for the chicken bits, the food scraps, and then my mother used to boil
it up. My dad came in at all times, and he used to have his dinner on
a plate and it would be dried up no end. And he couldn't see very well
'cos we didn't have electricity where we were, it was all gas mantles.
And my dad came and ate what he thought was his dinner, but he'd
eaten the bits, and he said to my mother, "It was tasty that stew, but it
was full of little bits".*

Phyllis Haddacks was a domestic science teacher.

*Teaching cookery in wartime was not too easy. The very strict rationing
meant it was impossible to ask girls to bring ingredients from home,
and although we had some rations, these were in very short supply. We*

were allowed a meat ration. This worked in theory but not in practice. Our meat ration was from our bluff neighbour, Mr CJC, who would invariably greet me, cleaver in hand, with, "Now Phyllis, what do you want?" I'd tell him. But he'd say, "You can't have it. I'll let you have a 'pund' of sausage". I'd say, "A pound of sausage is no good to me". But he'd ignore me and shout to one of his staff, "Hamilton, a 'pund' of sausage for the lady. Goodbye Phyllis". If you meet any super sausage roll maker in York, ten to one she was one of my pupils.

Phyllis Haddacks, domestic science teacher at Scarcroft School (Lois Wilson)

Phyllis Haddacks, 2004 (Lois Wilson)

It wasn't only shortages that made cookery difficult. When the air raid sirens went, I was responsible for taking my class to the shelters and looking after them. Very often though, I had food in the oven which also needed my attention. Trying to decide where I was needed most was often quite tricky.

Mary Barnes recalls,

Rations were pretty grim. We had curious things to eat like whale meat. It was just like beef steak to look at. I wouldn't touch it now as I'm conservation minded. I didn't like it much, it was fishy. Another curious thing we had was macon. That was to help your bacon ration. Instead of it being made of pork, it was made of mutton, and it was quite reasonable. We used to make pastry with liquid paraffin at one time. There was very little fat you see. But the government stopped us doing that because it was supposed to be cancer forming. They said during the war we were more healthily fed than we are now, 'cos there was no junk food. We had to eat more fresh vegetables.

Food salvage van at Walney Road, Heworth (York Oral History Society)

Una Hiscoe recalls how queuing became part of the British psyche.

We used to queue up a lot to get food. I used to go with my mam. On Ouse Bridge there was Wright's butchers. Each Saturday morning we'd be there by seven o'clock queuing up.

Mabel Robson remembers

Everybody told one another when things were happening. You'd hear "Wright's have sausages", so hat and coat on and we used to run, it was right down near the Regent. [This was the Acomb branch]. Sometimes we got there and they'd sold out. Sometimes we got maybe two, used to bring them back and my little daughter had her dinner with her granny. Or we used to do toad in the hole to make it go further. But then next day we just had to have dried egg. We always seemed to manage somehow.

Lilian Faulkner was rather crafty.

I had a bicycle and I had a seat made for the little boy. We used to cycle about 20 miles out into the country, Malton Road way, and I got to know a lot of farms. We went round, "Have you got any eggs to spare?" They'd say, "Two or three", so I generally came back with two or three dozen eggs and anything else I could get. And I'd feed my family like that, and any surplus, I used to let the old age pensioners have them.

I came back once from Heslington village, I had a big pram and there was a leather bag on it, a shopping bag and a lid. In that bag I had nine dozen eggs all wrapped in newspaper. I'd been to every farm and got a few at each one. And there was a policeman walking along and he says, "Good afternoon". And we were talking and he says, "What have you got in the bag then?" I was dreading him asking that, so I says, "What would you say if it was full of eggs?" "I bet you wish it was", he said, and we were laughing. I'd told him the truth and he couldn't believe it. I saw him last year and he said, "You would've got ten years if I'd known". But if I hadn't have got them, somebody else would. I shared them out with everybody. Better than let people go hungry. You should have seen the light in an old person's eyes when she got a few fresh eggs.

Rose Mary Wilcox recalls,

You had to register with the milkman, the coalman, and we were registered at the Maypole Dairy. That was for butter, margarine, eggs, sugar and tea, the basic things that were rationed. Things like dried fruit and biscuits, I think you could get those at other shops if they had them. If you saw a queue you joined it. The adults would get on the end, hoping that it would be something they wanted. When my sister got older, you used to queue up for lipstick. They'd say, "Ooh the chemist has got lipsticks in", and there'd be a queue. But they'd probably only got a box of about a dozen and there'd be a queue of 30 or 40.

You had to register with a butcher, and they had offal, liver and kidneys, or sausage. It was up to how popular you were with the butcher. They'd only got so many. You might get two sausages with your meat ration as a big favour. You could get tins of spam and bully beef. It wasn't very nice. My dad was very funny. He liked meat on the hoof, he didn't like tins.

On the farm, [where she was evacuated], *they had rations, but if you're in the midst of plenty, you're not going to scrimp. They had their own vegetable garden, and plenty of fruit, they had an orchard. If they killed a pig, the pig had to go to a proper butcher to be killed and they said they didn't waste anything on the pig except the squeak, everything else was used, even the tail. I think the farmers had a very good war, looking back, and you can't blame them. I mean you're not going to give everything away to the Ministry of Food.*

My dad worked at Thorp Arch, they were building underground shelters for the RAF. And he used to go out shooting rabbits on a lunchtime. So we had a lot of rabbit. He used to swap two for a ham shank at the Maypole and swap two for an extra bag of coal with the coalman. He knew lots of people in the countryside. We didn't go short but we didn't have a lot of fancy stuff.

Mavis Morton's father had his own ways to feed his family.

He used to go to Kirkham Abbey and all the engine drivers were the same, they used to set snickles [snares] for rabbits. And mushrooms if they were in season. And he used to eat starling pie. He'd make a wooden frame with a net over the top and a cane up it with a piece of string till they used to come, with a false sense of security. One thing I couldn't eat was those starling pies, but my father enjoyed them.

Mabel Robson had a stroke of luck during the war. Her husband put their daughter's name into a charity raffle.

And she was one of the lucky ones. And people from South Africa sent us parcels. I wrote and thanked them and said I was so pleased to have them. There was butter and sugar, and a few woollies for the little girl and all sorts of oddments, and currants and sultanas. They used to send us a big tin of ham, and we all used to share it. And then I got this letter back saying I was the only one that had written and thanked them, so I was going to have a parcel every two months for the next two years.

Of course, the forces were exempt from severe rationing, and the Americans and Canadians seemed to be able to get almost anything as Joyce Wells explains,

I remember going to a meal at Sand Hutton Hall, the Canadians were there. I had a boyfriend in the Canadian army. It was the first time I'd seen ice cream. I've never seen such a spread in all my life. It was like fairyland, all this stuff the Canadians had got. We used to get sugar sometimes, his sisters used to send him sugar and he used to bring it for my mum. And candy, what we would call boiled sweets. I remember him bringing some chocolate once. And we thought it was great, 'cos sweets were on ration. But it was horrible. After being used to Rowntree's lovely smooth chocolate, it was real gritty, but we ate it!

Joyce worked at the station

*for the Ministry of Food. We had all the food for the forces. I'd bike
to work and we had a canteen. It was at one end of the platform, the
office was at the other end. They used to bring us our coffee up. She
used to say, "I'm making dripping toast this morning, how many do
you want?" And she had these great platefuls of dripping toast. I think
that must have kept me going. Everybody used to have it. I don't know
where she got all the dripping from, nobody asked.*

*We had to wait for trains coming in with the food in, for our fellas
to unload into the store. And I've had to go into work Saturday and
Sunday 'cos we had to do the paperwork and we've worked all weekend.
You daren't leave the siding full of the wagons in case there was an air
raid. We used to work some long hours.*

Joyce met her husband Stan Wells later in the war at the Ministry of
Food, as he was then delivering for them. He recalls,

*There was a lot of fat in the cold store, coming out of this beef, because
a lot of the stuff that was in there come from the Argentine, and a lot of
Australian beef. All these hind quarters, they had big lumps of suet in
them. And with it being frozen, it used to break out did this fat. When
you were handling a lot, you'd have two or three of these big lumps of
suet and didn't know which pieces they'd come out of. So you didn't go
through several hundred to try and find just where a piece of suet went.
They just used to put it into the canteen and she'd melt it down, that's
where dripping came from.*

When the meat was sent over,

*the hind end was cut off and the legs were cut off, and pushed with their
legs inside the carcase, telescoping them, and they used to telescope
the sheep as well, for packing, because a lot came from New Zealand,*

81

Australia, Argentine. A lot of sides of pork came in from America, frozen. I'd be driving a lot of this stuff and taking it out to army camps. Everywhere you went, especially before D-Day, all round York, anywhere where there was any spare ground it was taken up by the army and their equipment. We knew when D-Day came, because they just all set off moving down south. And when we saw them moving en masse like they did, we knew there was something going off.

Eating out was uncommon in wartime, especially for the working classes. The government authorised what were known as British (or Civic) Restaurants. They were government-run cheap eating places and York had ones at Aldwark, Burton Stone Lane, Falsgrave Crescent and St Chad's near the Knavesmire. The Acomb restaurant opened in 1943, and cooking for all the restaurants was then centralised at Aldwark, with meals being transported to the others. People working in factories and offices invariably had a staff canteen. During times when there were raids, there were emergency feeding centres set up at Cherry Street School off Bishopthorpe Road, and James Street Adult School, Heworth Church of England School and St Mary's Hall, Marygate. Mavis Morton went to one of the Civic restaurants.

There was one where the market is now. You could only go perhaps once a month, it was about ninepence or something. Even these people who could afford it, they could never exceed five shillings. There was always food to be had, I can honestly say I never starved during the war.

Lord Woolton became the Minister for Food in April 1940, and the government issued numerous leaflets and articles in magazines giving advice on how to make interesting meals, with some rather unusual recipes. Suggestions included mock hare soup, eggless salad dressing, sardine fritters, oatmeal and vegetable goulash, egg and rice loaf, baked cod with parsnip balls and stewed pig's trotters with caper sauce. Not to mention mock plum pudding, hard roe butter, oatmeal and herb sausages, rook pie with figgy paste and marrow surprise. There was even 'Woolton Pie', which consisted of potatoes, swedes, carrots, onions, parsley and oatmeal, vegetable extract, and a crust of pastry. The government's 'Grow More' Bulletin no 3 of May 1942 gave 26 pages of information on how to store, bottle and can fruit, and make preserves.

It was not just food that was rationed. Families were only allowed 75% of their previous consumption of gas, coal and electricity. New clothes of course were not freely available. As well as having the money to buy clothes, people also needed clothing coupons from 1941. The allocation was 66 per adult per year. A dress would need seven, a coat fourteen, shoes would take five, a jumper or blouse would take five, vests or bras or belts all required three coupons, gloves would only need two, but a suit required eighteen. Women wore trousers more and more, with socks, to keep stockings for special occasions. It is well known that when American troops came over in 1942, they brought supplies of nylons to charm the local girls.

When it came to a special event, like a wedding, everyone pooled what coupons they had and borrowed and begged from relations and friends. Before the war, 30,000 workers produced clothing. In 1941 there were 1500. In fact world production of man-made fibres fell by almost a half, and cotton by a third. The government introduced the Utility Scheme. A lot of goods, including clothes and even furniture, were made to a certain standard, with no unnecessary extras, and had to carry a label saying 'utility clothing' and the logo CC41. Suits and dresses for example did not have pockets, seams, stitching or adornment. The government also advertised 'Mrs Sew and Sew' who gave housewives advice on economic tailoring. There were renovation services too, where clothes could be altered or repaired. Those who could knit and sew were fortunate.

Avril Appleton's mother

made a lot of clothes. She was a good seamstress and I never had any bought clothes until I was about 16. I used to get hand me downs from my cousins, apart from my school uniforms. She was always sewing and knitting and we used to make bags out of milk bottle tops, like cardboard tops with a hole in them, we'd sew them all together and make raffia bags.

Nora Denby remembers

the first lot of nylons that came to one of the shops in York. There was queues about a mile long for these nylons. We all went and queued up and I hadn't a daughter then who was big enough to be getting towards nylon age, but she queued as well to get another pair for mum.

'Make Do and Mend' leaflet

I think they expected rationing to finish almost immediately but it went on for two or three years [after the end of the war]. *Things kept coming back, getting a bit more plentiful, but it was a long time before we finally finished with the ration books. My dressing gown wore out, so I had a big browny grey blanket and we cut this up and made new dressing gowns, one for me and one for my daughter.*

Rose Mary Wilcox learnt how to sew at school.

We used to have 'Make do and Mend' lessons, showing you how to use something else for another person. We'd be told to bring an old cardigan of your mum's and we'd make it into a bolero and do blanket stitch round. Clothing was so expensive and you'd got to have coupons. You were made to use everything you could and not waste anything. And there were jumble sales. If you could get a man's suit or a big skirt, you could unpick it and wash it and press it, and you could cut it out for something smaller. That came in handy when I had kids. It's a chuck away society now.

Maureen Jerrum's mother was able to improvise.

My mother used to be a seamstress for the army. When a new soldier went in and the uniform didn't fit him, they'd bring the uniforms up to my mother's house and she used to change the size or shorten. She was given the parachutes that were no use. All our confirmation dresses were made out of parachute silk [there were five girls]. *Our blouses for school were made. She washed them and did them up. She had a boiler in the back kitchen, she used to put material in and she made us black skirts to go to school. I don't know where she got the dye from. She utilised everything she possibly could.*

The manufacture of cosmetics was cut down to a quarter of its pre-war production, but Joan Sadler was quite innovative.

We had leg make up. You bought the stuff in a bottle and put it on with cotton wool, and if we were in late and couldn't be bothered to wash our legs, my mother used to go frantic with the sheets. Tights were unheard of in those days and you couldn't get stockings. You wanted it on fast so you could get out, and [if it rained] *it all seeped down your legs. You used to get Kirby grips and grip your hair and turn it up. I can't remember anybody colouring their hair. I guess the factories would be making more important things. When I go into Superdrug and see the selection of shampoos and conditioners, I mean you wouldn't have thought then, that it would be shelves full of stuff just to do your hair.*

Another thing in short supply was toys. Lilian Faulkner remembers Christmas 1944.

I had a boy who was four years old, there were no toys for them at Christmas. No sweets, and no oranges, apples or bananas. I remember going down Thief Lane and seeing an old pedal car in somebody's front garden with no front wheels, sort of dirty and neglected. I went to the door and said could I buy it and they said, "No, you can have it". I gave the little girl four and six which was a fortune in those days. I took it home and I went to Clancy's the scrap metal people and they found me an axle with two wheels that would go on the car. I took the whole lot to the garage and I went back a couple of days later and he said, "There it is". I said, "Where?" All I could see was a beautiful green and white car and you ought to have seen it. I brought it home and hid it away until Christmas. When he took it out, he said, "It won't go". I says, "Hey up petal, you put your feet on and pedal it". There must have been 40 children came round, they seemed to appear like the Pied Piper, just to stroke the car. It nearly made me cry though, we tried to give as many as we could rides on it. But this little car, he kept it for years, he was a king because he'd got this car.

There was a shop in town, Pickering's, and I knew the manager there. He said, "Do you want to buy a toy for Christmas?" I said, "Yes please". He said, "Well it's got 'Made in Germany' on it, I've had it for some time. If I put it out, I'll get my windows smashed". And it was a conjuring set.

BLACK MARKET

There was obviously a black market because people mention it, but there were very few prosecutions. In April 1941, a man was fined £5 for receiving stolen items, 1lb 3oz of tea, four tins of casserole steak, one tin of beans, two of salmon, three of pears and one of pineapple, together with six and a half dozen eggs. In the same year, a man was imprisoned for 14 days for supplying potatoes, which were 'not fit for human consumption'. In August 1943, a number of items were found in the hollow of a tree on Middlethorpe Ings, including dried milk, pilchards, sardines, mustard, crab paste, macaroni, coffee, vegetable soup and carrot soup. But there is no record of anyone being arrested for this. Because food provision was so important, receiving stolen food carried a high penalty. There were a few cases of heavy fines for people who stored petrol.

Doreen Bolton was landlady at the Royal Oak in Goodramgate during the war.

Coppers always used to come after time, when they were on t' beat, and I always remember one night, there was a real character at York, Seth. He was a rugby player and a butcher, he come in one day, and he had a bike with a big basket, what they used to deliver meat on, and he flew upstairs! And next thing two 'tecs [detectives] come in.

With that, Seth ran off. Doreen knew he had been up to something, and when she went upstairs, she made a strange discovery.

He'd run upstairs and put a pig in our bedroom, in my bed! Ooh they used to do some things, they did, honestly.

Eric Rayson fought in the army during the war, and was at Dunkirk, escaping with his life. He recalls meeting people later, who had made money on the black market.

They made fortunes, absolutely. I do know one that really made a lot of money, and he told me it was because of the war. He used to deal in gravel and things for making aerodrome runways. He had ten trucks and he used to take them on and they'd count the number of trucks so they could pay him accordingly. He said he took ten trucks on, full of the various stuff, then he'd run five out still loaded at the other end,

Eric Rayson 2005 (Van Wilson)

then come back with his supposed ten trucks again. And he said, "I was doubling up on my payment all the time," he said, "I did that all the war". I thought, "Well you deserve to be shot". They made fortunes on the black market, they made themselves very rich.

Another man, when they said, "What is your occupation?" He said, "I'm a market gardener". "Ah, you can't join up, you've got to plough the fields". "But I'm only small". "Oh don't worry, we'll give you the finance to buy more". Which they did. And he bought acres and acres and acres and grew nothing else but carrots, he made a fortune. A lot of people didn't give two hoots for the country anyway, all they wanted to do was to get out of the services.

But there were legal food clubs. There were pig clubs. You all contributed so much to keep a pig. In those days it was easy to keep a pig. Now they're very strictly controlled, thank goodness. Everybody would swill out muck and rubbish from the kitchen, "Give it to the pig". And that's how the pigs fed. Then the pig would grow up and they'd kill it and share it amongst the people.

Rubye Readhead remembers,

There was this man, used to come into the Starre, he'd bring in fob watches and silver watches on chains. You name it, he could get it. He was in Gloucester, and there were a lot of trees with mistletoe. Next time he came on leave, he called in, he had a little Ford 8 and he'd filled it with mistletoe and he paid peanuts. He sold it for half a crown a sprig. Beat that for enterprise.

CHAPTER SIX

THE YORK AIR RAIDS

During the Second World War, there were ten minor air raids on York, and a major one in April 1942, known as the 'York Blitz' or the 'Baedeker Raid'. The minor raids occurred early on in the war, four in 1940, three in 1941, and three in 1942, and casualties were low. York got off very lightly compared to other cities in the country like London, Birmingham, Coventry and Liverpool. (The worst hit place in Yorkshire was Hull where 1200 died in the raids, 3000 were injured and 152,000 made homeless).

Inspecting bomb damage at Beckfield Lane 1940 (York City Library)

Mabel Robson recalls walking down Carr Lane in Acomb, and witnessing the air raid in November 1940,

I heard the aeroplane and thought, "What a funny noise". There was a policeman coming down and all of a sudden there was gunfire. He just threw his bike down and threw me into the hedge. I was absolutely appalled and I told him off. I've laughed about it since but I didn't laugh at the time. It was terrible really. And there was gunfire on the houses down Beckfield Lane.

In fact there were no human deaths on that occasion, but a few animals died, and a number of houses were damaged.

Harold Welburn 2005
(Brian Freeborn)

Harold Welburn recalls a raid in January 1941 on the Groves area.

My father was driving for York Gas Company delivering coke and he would be coming up 40. As he got older he never got called up, I think because of his job, and he had a problem with his back, he was deferred.

We lived in Eldon Terrace. We didn't have an air raid shelter. The arrangement was that our next door neighbour, we'd go out of the back and use their shelter. They couldn't build a shelter at the end of the yard 'cos there was a reception chamber there for a sewage system, and it could have toxic fumes. We'd had three or four warnings prior to this, each time we'd go out and just sit there and wait half an hour or so, and there'd be an all clear and we'd just go back in. And this particular night, we could hear the siren going. My dad said, "Come on then". I said, "No I'm not going out, we've had all this bother before", and I just lay there in bed. And then I heard a plane, and then about five or six crumps, and flashes of light in the bedroom. So I got up quick and went out to the shelter.

I went to St Thomas's School in Lowther Street and a bomb had dropped behind the school, one in Brownlow Street, one somewhere further along, about five or so all in a line, and the last one on the gas works. One man was killed in Brownlow Street. There was a shop on the corner, a short road that led up to Park Grove School. He was coming downstairs and the bomb landed in his yard.

We had to leave St Thomas's temporarily while they repaired the school. When we went back to school, that wall was still damaged. And being a lad, instead of going down to Eldon Street, I went up Markham Street, down the lane, and climbed up the broken wall which was like a series of steps, walked along the top and came down in the schoolyard. And eventually the wall was built again.

Doreen Angus remembers an early raid.

We were running to the shelter, and we had to get my mother down the stairs and she wouldn't go into the shelter without the little leather bag which contained the insurance policies. And then an aircraft came very low and it was machine gunning. It hit the Co-op at Haxby with bullets. I think it was after the aerodrome at East Moor. The air raid warden was coming along and he said, "Get down", and we lay flat on our faces on Yearsley Bridge, and covered our heads while this thing had gone over. When we got up we couldn't find him, but we dashed straight in, and he was sat there smoking his pipe quite happily!!

Tony Wood recalls an air raid in August 1942, which involved his father's business.

I was playing golf with my father, during the summer holidays, and I noticed a Junkers 88 flying over the golf course. You must understand that as a small boy we all had interests in that sort of thing, and I thought I was pretty good at aircraft recognition. It turned out that I was right on this occasion because a minute later there was a large crump in the distance, and then shortly afterwards somebody came rushing out to my father to say he was wanted urgently back in his business in York. A bomb had fallen on Queen's Staith right alongside his warehouses, and so actually my aircraft recognition had been right on this occasion. But it was quite a shattering thought actually.

400 properties were damaged during this particular raid. Peter Goater was nearby at the time.

I used to do a lot of rowing. We were in a double sculler, and what we used to do was go from Ouse Bridge up the river nearly to the palace [at Bishopthorpe] *and turn round. You had to time yourself, but as we were coming back, me and my pal, we had our backs to the town but his younger brother was steering, he was facing. He said, "Ooh, there's an aeroplane dropping parcels". And it was obviously King's Staith, opposite the pub, on that warehouse, that's what they hit. We immediately, when we heard the 'boom, boom', pulled into the shore on the first Fulford field, got out of the boat, ran onto the grass, and laid down. We saw the plane come over and we could see the rear gunner, his helmet and his goggles. I think it was a Junkers 88.*

Sheila and Peter Goater, 2001 (Sheila Goater)

Peter and Sheila Goater did not actually meet until after the war, but strangely enough had similar experiences early on in the war. It was probably the same occasion when Sheila had

gone up the river in a canoe with two friends, they lived near us, a sister and brother, and we went and camped overnight somewhere up near Poppleton. We suddenly heard this 'boom, boom', these two bombs that were dropped. We thought they were just getting rid of these bombs after they'd been somewhere else.

York citizens were told, 'If you are caught in the street when bombs are falling, drop flat on your face, taking advantage of the protection afforded by low garden walls, stationary vehicles or even the kerbstone'.

John Birch was 17 when the war began, and working for the building firm Birch and Son. He was also in the Home Guard. He recalls the raid of 17 December 1942, when the firewatchers were unprepared.

It would be about ten o'clock at night because the pub was still open, and I know for a fact there'd be a couple of them in the pub. It was known as 'The Firewatchers' Arms'. I think they called it the Ebor Vaults, right on the corner where the Merchant Taylors' is, in Aldwark. But I was in Layerthorpe at the time with my wife. And then when that bomb went, I went down to Fawdington Lane, where the gas company houses are.

The gas works had been hit by both incendiary bombs and heavy explosives, with several unexploded bombs close by. Fortunately only two people were killed, but 25 were injured. John continues,

The shrapnel must have pierced the tank, [the gasholder]. I can remember seeing the flames coming out and there was Charlie Foster and Tommy Wrigglesworth up the ladder plugging the holes. It did

knock so much of the guard room down. Just as you come out of what is now Sainsbury's, there was the gates and then Charles Foster's house was at the other side. There was always a policeman stood on duty there, on them gates. Afterwards we moved to the guard room at the other side of the river, where the contaminated land is. The smell was terrible there.

Harold Welburn describes the same incident.

The bomb hit Foss Bank, which is now Sainsbury's and Homebase, quite close to the roundabout area, that was the gas works entrance. There was a big office, there was a laboratory and at the end was another room used as the post for the Gas Company Home Guard which my father was in. And the bomb landed on that. My father should have been on duty that night but he took the evening off. There were several Home Guard on duty, but the pub, the Brigadier Gerard, *was the Gasworks Social Club. So nobody was in that guard room.*

THE BAEDEKER RAID

The 'Baedeker' raids were in retaliation for the bombing of Lübeck and Rostock in March and April 1942, which caused over 1000 deaths and massive destruction. Immediately after those raids, Hitler decided to systematically bomb cathedral cities in England, using the German Baedeker guide book for reference. Within two weeks, Exeter, Bath, Norwich and York were hit, with Canterbury affected the following month. Although some cathedrals had been badly damaged by the German Luftwaffe, including Coventry, Manchester, Exeter, and of course St Paul's in London, though damage there was internal, York Minster was left untouched, probably because it served as a good reference point from the air.

The York Baedeker Raid occurred in the early hours of 29th April 1942, when over 70 German aircraft followed the River Ouse into the

War damage outside Tower Cinema, New Street, April 1942 (York Oral History Society)

city, aiming for the station, which was a very important railway junction on the line from Scotland to London. And of course many troops passed through the city. The bombers came in over the North Sea and hit Clifton, Bootham, Wigginton Road, the city centre (where the Guildhall in particular was burnt out, and the church of St Martin's in Coney Street was badly damaged), the station, Leeman Road, then the Nunnery Lane/Scarcroft area, and on into Acomb and Poppleton Road. Tang Hall and Fulford were also hit. Unfortunately the sirens did not sound until it was too late for many, the planes were already overhead. 92 civilians were killed, and 204 injured that night, with an unknown number of casualties from the forces. The only allied airman who came to the rescue was French pilot, Yves Mahé, flying a Hurricane. He managed to shoot down one of the Heinkel aircraft. He received the French Croix de Guerre and a hero's welcome at the Mansion House after the war.

The attack had devastating results and wardens and rescue workers toiled for hours to dig out those who were trapped, with little thought for their own safety, as Frank Fox recounts in chapter 3.

Phyllis Haddacks was a teacher at Scarcroft School at the bottom of Moss Street.

I was on fire-watching duty on the night the air raid began. I'm no heroine but I can't recall feeling afraid. There seemed too much to do. Walking casualties and people suffering from shock were brought into the ARP shelter in Moss Street. I made hot drinks from my domestic science room which wasn't easy as we could have no light on, as the room was not fitted with blinds or curtains. All domestic science teachers had been allocated a centre at which we were to get water for brewing tea. This was in case homeless people were brought in. I had been given Poppleton Road School so when the bombing ceased, I cycled off up Moss Street and there met someone who asked me, "Where do you think you're going, Phyllis?" I said, "Poppy Road School". And she said, "Well you needn't bother, it had a direct hit". I thought I must do something, so I set off for Haxby Road School. I passed the station where there were firefighters, hoses and mountains of shattered glass. I had to pick up my cycle and carry it over all this impedimenta. I put the boilers on at Haxby Road and waited, but happily no homeless came. I then pedalled home for a wash and brush up. I found mother in tears, she'd been told it was Scarcroft School that had been hit and she'd been saying, "Phyllis was always such a good girl". She soon got over that and things returned to normal. Wash and brush up completed, I cycled off back to school ready for teaching. I'd just taken off my coat when the headmaster came in and said, "Isn't it sad about Betty Ankers?" I asked why and he said, "She was killed last night". My legs really turned to jelly and the night's events became a reality. She was one of my little twelve year olds. I took some of her friends to the funeral and I can still feel the way they clung to me and wept. Man's inhumanity to man.

John McElheran remembers the raid.

*Our house in Sycamore Terrace, near Scarborough Bridge, was badly
damaged by a bomb which fell uncomfortably near and killed one man.
My father stood in the back lane protected by his tin hat watching the
railway burn. My pregnant mother urged him to join us in the air raid
shelter he had built in the back garden. The Valor gas stove jumped up
and down when the bombs fell. My mother remarked that she supposed
it (the stove) was rather dangerous! The bombs whistled and there
was machine gun fire which left bullets in the bath. The following day,
as my father cleaned the ceiling out of the piano which he had left the
previous evening with all its lids removed for tuning, we were taken
away to New Earswick by friends who had come to see how we were.
We were only away for a few days but we had no ceilings and there was
canvas for some time where the windows had been, and a hole in the
roof. A neighbour, not a house-proud woman at the best of times, was
still attributing the grime in her house on 'the Blitz' seven years later.
It was a local joke!*

John Scott recalls

*the sirens sounding night after night and hearing the German bombers
going over York heading for the docks in Liverpool. We spent many
hours sitting in our brick air raid shelter at the bottom of the garden
with a candle burning in a plant pot. Father had got hold of three tin
helmets and we put them on.*

*In April 1942 everybody was asleep in bed. In the early hours of the
morning, bombs started to fall. We dived into the front room and
the safest place was to be by the chimney breast. Next morning they
sounded the all clear and we all gathered at the top of Scarcroft Hill and
we could see York burning. Two ladies next door had fortified themselves with a bottle of whisky and were dancing round in the street. My*

school had disappeared, it was all rubble. Eventually a letter arrived and said I had to report to a girls' school in Priory Street.

John Scott (in centre) with two fellow soldiers (John Scott)
John Scott, 2005 (Mike Race)

Tony Wood was also a schoolboy in 1942.

I remember actually spending half the night under the kitchen table. I went to St Olave's School and I used to go in by bus but I seem to remember that nothing got in the way of school. It was a bit smelly and there was quite a bit of fire damage around Bootham.

John Mennell joined the ARP as a messenger boy when he was 16 in 1941.

On the night of the air raid, I had to report to the warden's base oppo-site the Odeon. It was downstairs at a cycle shop called Shearsmith's. One of the first bombs was on the Bar Convent. Being the nearest ARP place, we rushed down, and I helped to get some of the nuns and the pupils through the coal chute down Nunnery Lane. We took them to a shop across the road, Rank's butchers, and then to a chemist on the other side of the road, called Parker's. The people were all awake and

John Mennell, 2005
(Van Wilson)

John Mennell as young man
(John Mennell)

standing outside. It's still there is the coal chute, a little door on the right hand side, down Nunnery Lane. Then they said, "John, you must take a message to the Guildhall to get troops 'cos we think there's more trapped". So I cycled past the station, that was ablaze, and when I got down to the Guildhall, that was all in blaze, so they redirected me to the War Office down Fishergate. As I was coming out, they were bringing in a German airman, he'd bailed out, I believe, at Naburn.

I went straight to work the following morning. People just had to carry on naturally. I carried on being a messenger boy until I was called up when I was 17¾ and I volunteered for the RAF and I finished up in Burma.

Tragically there were five nuns who didn't get out of the Bar Convent. Kate Houghton went to Mill Mount School and remembers

I was going to school and I walked up Nunnery Lane just as they were bringing the bodies out of the nuns. Later on, one of my friends and I were in Coney Street, and I can feel it now, the crunching of the glass at St Martin's.

Joan Pannett worked at the Carriageworks and remembers the air raid.

That was terrible 'cos we were on nights. There wan't half some bangs, they were up and down the railway lines. It frightened us to death, and we all had to dash out and into the shelters. When we went home, my mum and dad were in the cupboard under the stairs and my mum couldn't stop shaking. My dad had had his leg off, so he'd had to put his [false] leg on to come downstairs. They were not injured but they [the planes] had peppered all the window sills as they went along. My eldest brother who lived in Leeman Road, walked in, in an old coat with some band tied round it. He'd been fire fighting at Leeman Road on the railway, and he'd been bombed. They got his wife out and his mother and father in law and his two daughters, but their handbags and their shoes were three streets away up on somebody's roof. [They lost] every possession they had. All my sisters who were married, they all rallied round until he got some compensation to live somewhere else.

Lilian Faulkner recalls another result of the bomb.

I was in the hairdresser's and the lady in the next chair, a girl about 20, said, "Our house was bombed last night". She woke up and, "I went to put my feet out of the bed and something made me stop. I heard a bang. If I had put my feet out, they would have gone straight through a hole in the floor into the room below, because the bang was the door dropping over the hole". She got out of bed and there was a baby in the room next to her in a cot and she couldn't see as it was pitch dark. She found her way to the other bedroom where her mother was, who said, "I'm caught, I'm trapped". A beam had fallen across her legs and the kiddie

*Bar Convent after
1942 air raid (York
Oral History
Society)*

*who was in the bed with her was safe because it was shorter. The baby
had been hit with a piece of brick and it had knocked it unconscious but
it was all right. When you hear of things like that, it makes you think
how lucky you've been. And do you know, somebody stole the stair
carpet in that house?*

Peter Goater recalls,

They dropped incendiaries on the old County Hospital and they landed on the verandah. The nurses were kicking them off, 20 or 30 of them, into the open space. They were quite light, only thin, but they were fizzing. We could look across there from Foss Islands. I thought, "Those nurses want a medal".

Peter Binns was nine that year.

My father worked at the old County Hospital and he used to do fire-watching duties. If he was at home on a night when the sirens went off, if it was obvious that they weren't bombing York, we used to go into the back yard to see if you could see anything. We had two air raid shelters built, one in the back yard, a brick shelter with a concrete roof and a steel door, for us to go in if there was an air raid. But because that was damp, my mum and dad had the cupboard under the stairs altered. Basically all that was done was supporting the stairs with pieces of three by two to make it stronger. And we used that as an indoor shelter because it was warm, it was dry, and we didn't have to go dashing down the back yard. We used to put on these siren suits which were like a pair of overalls made of blanket type material to keep you warm over your pyjamas.

My dad went outside and said, "Come and have a look at this". And we went down to the end of the back yard and the whole of Clifton Ings was on fire with incendiary bombs. It was just like a continuous flash gun. And then the planes were coming over and somebody started machine gunning. My dad says, "Right, time we went inside". You could hear bombs whistling down and pots rattling in the cupboards, and then next thing, you could hear this whistling but it was a different sound. And then everything went absolutely quiet, probably only for about a second, and then bang, that was it. The roof came down, the walls fell in, the windows went out. The bomb had landed on the other side of the street and it had demolished some terraced houses, and because things were that unsafe and you couldn't breathe for the brick dust, my dad decided to go for the shelter in the yard. So it was a case of me under one arm, my sister under the other one, shouting at my mum, "Come on Doris". We got into the shelter and Dad then went to have a look if Mr and Mrs Cook were all right, 'cos they had a similar sort of shelter. I remember saying to my dad, "I wonder if Wilf's all right". Wilf Feetenby was a lad I used to play with, four doors away. And he went down there and then, "Yeah, the Feetenbys are all right. They're trapped but they're working on it to get them out". And going the other way up the street, Mr Johnson who lived next door, he got some shrapnel in his leg. So my mum, being a first aider, went to dress his leg. And we basically sat there until the all clear went, which was almost daylight.

And when you step outside and you see that your house that was there when you went to bed, was no longer there, it's a bit of a shock. Until then, it used to be fun in one sense, putting your gas mask on when you were at school. If the siren went off during the night, you used to be able

Peter Binns, 2005 (Van Wilson)

Peter Binns as young man in York Radio Relay van (Peter Binns)

*to skip the following morning's school and go in at lunchtime. For a
kiddie of my age, it was fun. You didn't realise something would happen.*

*But when we saw it the following morning and the house had gone,
and the furniture was all in pieces, and your toys, they'd all gone, they
were under piles of rubble, it really comes home to you what war is
about. My dad went running round here, there and everywhere, to find
out what we could do. We finished off going up to a house which was
a bombed-out reception centre on Boroughbridge Road and they gave
us blankets and gave me a monopoly set which was an American one.
My mum's brother lived in Prior's Walk so we slept on their floor for
a few nights until we got sorted out. My mum used to do some part-
time work at a grocer's shop and we slept in their big lounge for quite a
number of weeks till my dad found a house to rent in Shirley Avenue.*

*I was allowed to go back and have a look at the house in the daytime.
The roof went off completely, the front wall had dropped down, and the
back floor had fallen out. The wall down the centre of the house was still
there and the back bedroom was hanging at an angle with my bed on
it, with the brass knobs on the top and a teddy bear above the bed. My
cousin Stephen went up and got that, he was older than me. My mum's
bed had a wood headboard top and bottom, and a wardrobe where all the
mirror was smashed. They used to take your furniture if it was salvage-
able, and store it for you and repair it. They had craftsmen and they'd
fill up all the shrapnel holes and then French polish it, and then when
you got your new house, you could get your furniture back. There was
a clock, and the Christmas decorations, they were in a cardboard box
which always used to sit on the top of the wardrobe in the front bedroom,
and she [his mother] opened the box expecting to find a box of glass,
'cos they were all glass ornaments in those days, and there wasn't one
broken.*

*My school, Poppy Road, got one right in the centre. After the raid, as
you walked up Lavender Grove, my mum said, "Look at your school". I*

Poppleton Road School after the air raid, 1942 (Yorkshire Gazette and Herald)

thought, "Oh no, all my little drawings on the wall have gone". But an hour or two afterwards, it struck you, you'd got no home. It was frightening. It's hard to describe. It's like you going home now and finding your house has disappeared and everything you've got has gone, clothes and everything. It makes you appreciate what you have. Basically my dad lost his house, he wouldn't have the money to have it rebuilt or buy another. Whatever money he'd saved was probably under the mattress in the front bedroom. If our house disappeared today, we can go to the bank, we can draw some money out and stay in a hotel for a week, whereas in those days you couldn't unless you were really rich.

Alwyn Banks had to go to Poppleton Road School in the capacity of his work as an electrician for the council.

We had to turn out to draw all the fuses so that the firemen could get their hoses onto it. In the mains box, if you pull the fuses out, it means the electricity is dead in the building. There were electric cables every-where, and if they were live, the firemen couldn't put their hoses on without some explosion or electrocution.

Winnie Mothersdale and her mother, who lived in Holgate, sheltered in the cupboard under the stairs.

We could see flashes and banging and that sort of thing, but then a bomb dropped right outside our house. You don't hear the whining, there's just this thud and you felt as though we were in a giant vacuum, it was a terrible feeling. The living room window came in and we had shut the cupboard, and the door opposite came off, and that banged into the cupboard, and the door leading out into the back yard came off and fastened us in. The stairs were all around our necks.

Then came the all clear, and I said to mother, "Don't move because we might bring something down". We could hear people walking about on slates and crunching and people shouting, "Anybody there? Anybody there?" So I said to mother, "Let's both shout together as loud as ever we can", which we did. Then, "Right-o, don't worry, we'll soon have you out", It seemed a long time. It was all black. The men said, "You'll have to climb very high up till you get to the top and then there'll be somebody at the other side will help you down". They were all very helpful and the curate of St Paul's, the Rev Sidney Smith, he was round doing what he could. He said, "Anybody who wants a cup of tea, I've got to take you to Mrs Pickering's". She was the only one with any water so she was making cups of tea non-stop. She had put her name down to take evacuees and she said, "I think if you and Winnie would like to stay with us until you find somewhere, at my age I think I'm a little bit past children". So we stayed there until we heard of this house in Linton Street.

Les Benson recalls

*During the raid, when the
Exhibition Building was
burning at the back of the Art
Gallery, this man worked for
the Selby telephone and cable
company, doing all the cables
for airfields. They kept their
wagons in there and he drove
them out into Marygate and
about a fortnight later the firm
awarded him £25 or something
for saving the wagons, which
was a fortune!! And the police
were gonna prosecute him for
not having a driving licence!*

Charles Minter was the City
Engineer, based at the Guildhall.

*They were restoring the
Guildhall, my own people, and
we'd nearly got it finished. We
had Archbishop Temple lined
up to open it and a fire bomb*

*Charles Minter, City Engineer, at a civic
occasion, 1936
(York Oral History Society)*

*dropped and set it on fire and it was spreading fast. One of my chaps
came in and we got the drawings out as much as we could, out of the
drawing office. We went through my office into this committee room
and there was a lot of wind about, and the door slammed behind us
and there was a latch on it and we couldn't get back. We saw the blaze
and we put tin hats on and made a run for it right across the front. We
got molten lead on our hats and backs, but we didn't get hurt. The fire
brigade came and the roof burnt off, and that was that. Later, General*

Bartholomew came along and I went out with the Superintendent of Works to see the damage near the Mansion House. And we went down into Leeman Road where they got a crater in the middle of the cross-roads and when we got there, there was this party on the other side of the road, the Commissioner, the Princess Royal and everybody else. He shouted across to me, "Come over here". So I went over and he introduced me to the Princess Royal and he said, "This is the City Engineer, ma'am, he gets on with the job and argues the point afterwards". That was how it went.

When the air raid came and the damage was done, they began to get a bit worried and they'd got a lot of very fine oil paintings, portraits, in the Mansion House. They told me to get them out and put them in a safe place. At the Castle Museum, in line with the Law courts, outside the Debtor's Prison, there's an opening about four feet wide, and some brickwork. We took those pictures down there and then threw them all in this opening. I was there with one of our bricklayers and after dark, I was helping them knock up the mortar and concrete and bricks, and we bricked it all up. That's where they stayed through all the war. They weren't packed by an expert but when they were taken out, they weren't damaged at all. And the City Plate, I went with the Sheriff to Harewood House, the Princess Royal said we could take it there, put it in their vaults. That's where that stayed all through the war.

Some of the panes of stained glass from the Minster, including six panels from the Five Sisters window, had been removed in August 1939 to a place of safety.

Lilian Roberts recalls

From our bedroom window we looked out on Rowntree's factory, and you could see a whole ring of lights. Just as if somebody had gone up in the sky on a ladder and hung chandeliers.

Sheila Goater remembers

Father worked at Ben Johnson's when they were in North Street. They had a shop and they sold typewriters and he was in charge of that part. The night of the Blitz, we were in the house, my mother and sister and I, he was out firewatching. When he came back in the morning, he said he was terrified. It must have brought it back, the bombing, the trench warfare in the First World War. The siren had gone that night and we hadn't bothered. My mother appeared at the bedroom door and she said, "I think you better get up". The planes were coming over us. We looked out of the window, they were gunning, there were bullets leaping off the roofs of the houses in the next road. So we dashed down the stairs. We had to go under the stairs, that's where we were aiming for. We'd only got into the passage beside the cupboard and the bombs were dropping round us and we just clung together until it stopped. How long it went on, I don't know, it seemed just terrifying. All the ceilings had come down and we were all covered in soot.

The bed that I was sleeping in, the whole window fell out over the bed. Good job I wasn't in it. The police advised everybody to go away that night. They had to take out all the furniture. Whitby Oliver stored it till the house was repaired. This was April. It would be the summer holidays before we got back in. It took time for them to come round and repair the windows and ceilings.

My mother and sister went to stay with a friend in Gillygate. My father wouldn't leave the house at all. I was a student at Leeds University so I went and stayed with my grandmother there. One particular person I remember hearing about, was someone who had a shop along Bootham. A man there had a grocery shop and he just disappeared. He was out firewatching and never seen again. And then a family who lived in Bootham Crescent, the children we were at school with, they were all killed.

Peter Goater explains that

The night they came it was beautiful moonlight, they could have bombed the Minster and they didn't, they kept away from it. The night after, on the radio there was Lord Haw Haw, William Joyce, [the German propagandist] *and he said, "People of York will wonder why we haven't bombed their beautiful Minster; the reason why is because the Führer is going to give his Christmas message from York Minster"!*

Official reports were quick to praise all those who had worked stead-fastly during and after the raid, the ambulance men and women, medical staff at the hospital, control and telephone room staff, civil defence wardens and firemen, even the Lord Mayor, Mrs Edna Crichton, who worked flat out for 18 hours superintending first aid posts, visiting the injured, and organising arrangements. She was called an 'inspiration to the citizens'. There was a real sense of community spirit and ordinary people were wonderfully supportive, helping in any way they could, lending their cars to get people to hospital, allowing use of telephones where they had them (many were put out of order during the raid), helping dig out those under the wreckage, taking in the homeless, and making endless cups of tea.

Others lent blankets, and also put their homes at the disposal of first aid workers, doctors, and bomb victims to wash and clean themselves up. A lot of people were suffering from shock and even one or two had heart attacks as a result. And of course the dead had to be laid out. The following day's *Yorkshire Evening Press* stated, "Coolness and courage under fire characterised the citizens of York last night, when the city underwent the ordeal of what was described by the Germans as a reprisal". Despite the attack on the station, by the following day, 75 per cent of the trains were running.

Brenda Milner has her own story to tell of that fateful night.

My father worked on the station and was on duty, it was usually eight in the evening until six the next morning. So my mother and I were in the house and we used to get lots of sirens and sometimes we'd get up and sometimes we wouldn't. But I remember my mother banging on the bedroom wall and saying, "Come on, they're here". People half expected York to be bombed that night because some of the other cathedral cities had been bombed. We had an

Brenda Milner 2005 (Van Wilson)

air raid shelter in the garden, one of the Anderson shelters which was a metal one. It usually had several feet of water in it 'cos the soil was very clayey where we lived so that was no good. We sat under the table with my budgie in his cage and stayed there until the all-clear went. This was in Heworth but we could hear it in the town, lots of noises and planes. And my father should have been home after it was all clear. When my father hadn't come back by eight, my mother thought she'd better go down to the station and see what she could. And sadly, they hadn't found him at that stage, but she went up onto the bridge over the railway lines and looked down and the buildings were all demolished. Apparently a train had come in with lots of passengers and they asked them to go down into the subways. And the station had a glass roof, that's what caused a lot of the damage, that collapsing and the glass breaking. Somebody had been injured, I think probably with broken glass, and my father must have decided to go back to his office to collect his first aid equipment. And unfortunately the building caught fire and collapsed on top of him so it was some time before they found his body.

During the time he was missing, one of the neighbours very kindly got on her bicycle and went round all the hospitals to see if he might be there. But he wasn't of course. And he could only be identified by the St John's Ambulance chain he wore as a watch chain. Every year the St

St John's Ambulance chain, belonging to William Milner. Each link represents a period of service. (Brenda Milner)

John's Ambulance people had to take an examination to qualify, and they got a little silver plaque which joined together could form a watch chain.

I was thirteen. I was at Queen Anne's School and the school had had a bomb in the grounds and all the windows were blown out. So for a few weeks, we were sent to Mill Mount School and Nunthorpe School alternately. At the Christmas following, presumably because I'd lost my father in the air raid, I received a parcel from some American charity, a rather nice red necklace, a sort of string of roses.

At the same time, my mother's sister who lived in Leeman Road, which was very badly bombed, lost her home. Her husband was in the army, so she and her two small sons came and lived with my mother for a couple of years. I was an only child, used to being on my own, so it was nice to have a couple of brothers for a short time. They were both pretty cheerful souls, in fact after that, we were given a Morrison air raid shelter, which was a table type in the living room. And I can remember Auntie Lily, when we were in there during an air raid, we had to sing very loudly, "She'll be coming round the mountains". She must have thought that we wouldn't hear the bombs.

Some time later, Brenda's mother, in memory of her husband, received the Civil Defence Brave Conduct medal, the King's medal. She continues,

There's a book with all the people who were killed in the air raid, in the church in Coney Street, St Martin's. His name's in there. I have been to a memorial service in there, 50 years after the air raid.

When the station was being modernised, they decided to build a waiting room on the site of the office where my father had worked and been

Brenda Milner unveiling plaque to her father, William Milner, at York Station, 1984 (Brenda Milner)

killed. So they put up a plaque in his memory which I unveiled in 1984.
A couple of years later, I happened to be Lady Mayoress when the Prin-
cess Royal came to the station to name a train. And it was decided that
I better show her my father's plaque and explain all about it. So that
was a great honour.

The rather moving postscript to this story, is that one of the German
pilots who bombed York on that night in 1942, Willi Schludecker, who
is now 87, returned here in 2007 to 'say sorry to the people of York'. He
met with Brenda and she said that she no longer felt any bitterness or
anger but was able to forgive, as our air force was doing the same to
the Germans.

Evelyn Hudson recalls the morning after the raid,

My friend Sheila and I got our pushbikes out and we cycled right up to
Nessgate. There was ambulances, fire, police all over the place, hose-
pipes right across the road. The church in Coney Street was blazing, the
Guildhall was blazing, but the road itself looked magnificent because
the glass from the church and from all the shops, it was embedded in the
tar and it was just like diamonds. It was unbelievable, and it was like
that for quite a few years because the tar was melted and it just sunk in
and it was like a mosaic all the way along Coney Street. There were no
windows in Kathleen Benson's [the hairdresser where she worked],
or the bank underneath. When I did go to work at half past eight that
morning we'd no gas, no electric, no water, but Terry's Restaurant
was opposite, and they had gas, electric and water, they'd never lost
theirs. They'd no windows, no roof, but the kitchen staff were very
good, coming out with trays of tea and coffee, for the firemen and the
police and any of the workers. But it was a weird morning, was that,
because for a long time everything seemed so quiet, so still, people just
wandering about and wondering.

CHAPTER SEVEN
WORK IN WARTIME

Many of the people who worked on the home front were plunged into quite difficult jobs, often heavy work, for long hours and poor pay. They were often very young, many straight from school, but they all seemed determined to do their bit 'for the war effort'. By April 1940, unemployment in York had dropped by 382,000.

FACTORIES

During the war, many factories changed their production to encompass munitions. Most of the production was carried out by women. Often they would make small component parts for aircraft, ships and tanks, not really knowing what they were for, but their role was very significant. They were, in fact, indispensable to the war effort.

Rowntree's was normally a chocolate manufacturer, and production continued to a lesser extent, but much of the output was for the troops. There was a separate department which was used for munitions. 60 men worked in this area, alongside 850 women! The work was so important that the employers tried to help in any way they could, which included providing a crèche for young pre-school children.

Sheila White worked at the factory.

I used to make half pound blocks of chocolate for prisoners of war. You put the chocolate at the side of the machine, we used to wrap and foil and then it went to the other department and they used to bitumen wrap, like a brown paper with a line of black in, so it wouldn't deteriorate. They'd send them to POWs through the Red Cross. You'd have to lift one, it was like a zinc bath with about a stone of chocolate in them. It was very tiring, it was men's work. I lost 12 pound while I was doing

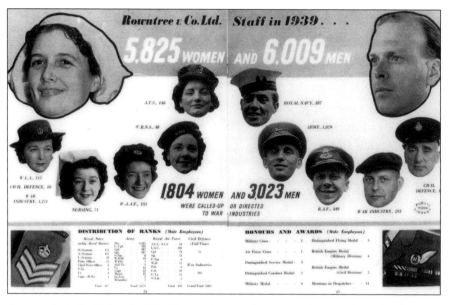

Rowntree's staff called up in 1939. Doreen Angus, who recounts her experiences in chapter four, is on the far left. (York Oral History Society)

that. The chocolate they made was special. They could only eat it on an officer's release. They could put a square in a cup of water and drink it, it was full of vitamins. White chocolate was for the troops, it had milk and cream in it. You couldn't eat too much of it, it was a food really, it was like eating Oxo. Then we did Lifeboat Naps, little Napoleon chocolates for submarines and the navy.

As well as the vitaminised plain chocolate, for army rations and starving children in Europe, the factory also made blended chocolate for prisoner of war parcels, Pacific and Jungle chocolate made to withstand high temperatures for armies in tropical climates, Oatmeal Block and Fruit Bar for men in Far Eastern theatres of war, and field ration chocolate used by the American forces. The army emergency rations were hermetically sealed in tins, and some were specifically for use in parachute operations.

The part of the factory which made shells was given the name of County Industries, and was located in the Smarties block of the Gum Department. The department also made jam and marmalade for Frank Cooper of Oxford, as authorised by the Ministry of Food. Part of the Almond Department was used by Cooke, Troughton and Sims for the expansion of their optical instrument work. The Card Box Mill which normally made chocolate boxes, was used by the RASC, Royal Army Service Corps, as a supply depot. The sawmill was where fuse packing cases were made, and White Tile Heaters took over part of this area to produce sea markers, flame floats and land mines. The Cream Department produced national milk cocoa for schoolchildren, Ryvita and dried eggs. Part of the factory offices was used by the 300 clerks attached to the Royal Army Pay Corps. Most of the cocoa was actually produced at a small mill in Walsden, a town on the Pennines.

County Industries March 1943, munitions department at Rowntree's
(York Oral History Society)

Mavis Morton

> *did Ryvita, it was on the fifth floor. And we used to do 7lb tins of emergency rations. We made sure they were airtight. There was this thing full of water, you put this tin in, and a glass on top, if there was an air bubble came off you just marked it, and somebody soldered and tested it again. We did this beautiful chocolate for prisoners, I did have a piece but we weren't supposed to eat it. We had to make the minimum amount of bars so we probably had one bar between us all, just to taste it.*

Sheila White recalls the women who worked in the munitions area.

> *The fuse fillers, the stuff used to stain their skin, it was all yellow. They wore brown overalls right up to the neck. They didn't have their food with us.*

There was special face powder and cream available for the workers, but it did not completely prevent the problem. They also drank milk at their breaks rather than tea or coffee. Maurice Kershaw remembers how this work began.

Women at Rowntree's making munitions (York Oral History Society)

Rowntree's was a food factory and therefore they had a certain number of staff who were reserved, and other people who were on the benches and the factory floor. Unless they were on a certain kind of work, for instance cocoa, they could be moved to other firms or work of national importance. The people from the Royal Ordnance Factory at Chorley in Lancashire came to see us. The first thing they said was, "We want to do it in this big block". We said, "We're going to do it on a main production line in units down the conveyor". Well they almost fainted 'cos those kinds of things always used to be filled in little huts, no more than 12 people in a hut, so if one explodes it kills 12 people not 250. Before we started, two or three of us that were going to look after the job, went to Chorley. There were all little huts mounded up with earth. They couldn't think that we could do this on main production lines like packing a box of chocolates. That shook them a bit. Secondly of course we were in a fortunate position that we had a lot of Rowntree girls chocolate packers, probably a quarter of our staff, a number of people who could teach others and had quite a lot of dexterity in their fingers.

We didn't put any powder in [the fuses], it was all detonation. The shells were what's known as percussion shells. We got the shells and we put the detonators in, which armed it. We started off with a target of 100,000 a week and we worked ourselves out of the job because our staff were packing 160,000. We didn't do that the first week or two, but eventually worked up to that. Finally we were doing so many, more than they wanted, and that was the end of us. I'm fairly qualified to tell you about this because I was the first person in the place. Well there was the manager, Sparks, and I was responsible for the office staff, and I was the chap who had to plan the delivery of fuses and parts for assembly, obtain the flow into the factory of detonation and powder.

The powder came from one of the Royal Ordnance Factories at Chorley. I don't think we had anything like that in Yorkshire. The fuses came from Doncaster. They were a firm who do castings and they went down the Don and then came up the Ouse by water. During that time the

*railways were pretty busy and these were just the right things to carry.
If you'd come in by train, you was pulling north and loading them
into the wagon, then you had to take them in a lorry to the Doncaster
loading bays for the goods train. Goods train got to York, you had to get
a lorry to bring them up to the factory, whereas crossing by waterway,
they put them on the barges, they came up the river and we unloaded
them.*

*Have you handed in your contraband? Munitions department at Rowntree's
(York Oral History Society)*

*In the reception area, it said, "Have you handed in your contraband?"
It was matches, cigarettes, tobacco, anything that could cause an explosion. You had to have rubber overshoes on. If I wanted a smoke, I used
to go down and pick me cigarettes up and have a smoke on the way
down. My actual job was like a purchase and distribution of the things,
I had to notify when the things were packed into boxes, and were going
back to the ordnance factory. They used to test these things on South-*

port sands. They only tested random samples and we got a reply saying that the batch had 'planned', and we could forget about that one, that was how that was done. In the whole of the time we were working there, in 2½ years, the only accident we had was a girl who was putting detonators into the fuses and she had a long fingernail, and she scratched the detonator and that didn't do her fingers any good. The detonator, it's only a tiny thing but it actually took her fingers off.

There was roughly 80 people on each unit and we had eight units. Four units on and four units off, day and night. They changed over every week. It was quite an interesting occupation. The girls put the fuses in trays, then they put them in the boxes, when they'd been filled. The men were on mostly transport. The last fuse was number 7,809,579. We were on this job roughly halfway into 1940 and finished at the end of 1941.

Rowntree worker filling the 7,809,579[th] *fuse in their munitions department. (York Oral History Society)*

Nancy Dawson also worked there and recalls how dangerous the job actually was.

We wore overalls and you couldn't have anything metal. You had to take all the hair grips out of your hair, and you could only wear a wedding ring, and then they taped it over with blue tape. And you were checked as you came into the cloakrooms. You put your overall on and your turban and before you could step over the barrier into the works room, there was a checker for metal. If you had glasses, with metal bits, they would tape them over. They used to call us the Yellow Perils, 'cos your hands and face used to go a yellowy colour.

This particular night I was tired 'cos I had been up early and had been out gadding, it was a job to keep my eyes open. I'd got my hands in

Nancy Dawson in ATS, later in war, in Ordnance Lane, second from right. (Nancy Dawson)

this machine and I'd nodded a couple of times, my head leant on this little box and there was a chargehand, and I'd nodded off and I heard somebody in my ear say, "Open your eyes and don't move your hands". Well I opened my eyes and lifted my head up. There was a little round brass piece with the detonator at one side, the hole at the other and I had it on the machine already for me to start stemming as they called it with the detonator upmost. If I'd have done it, the detonator would have gone off and blown my hand off, and I was asleep. She said, "Get downstairs to the toilets and wash your face in cold water and come back, and if you fall asleep again I'm sending you home". That one would have gone off because I would have touched it with this brass rod. It was awful if you felt tired when you were on nights. The sirens went many a night but you didn't go down to the shelters. We had our own warden, and if he gave you the red, which he did the particular night the bomb dropped, he gave the signal, get down to the shelters. If a bomb had hit even in the shelter, you wouldn't have stood a cat in hell's chance, with all these shells and detonators and everything. There would have been one almighty bang.

They had to go right across the Wigginton Road part of Rowntree's to an outbuilding where all the detonators were kept. Two of them went at a time. One in front carrying a little red flag to warn anybody and the other girl behind carrying the detonators.

When the sirens went this particular night, nobody took much notice. Then eventually we got the warning from the roof top that they really meant business. We were all congregated by the doorway and one or two of them were getting a bit hysterical. The overlooker came to me and said, "Will you get some singing going or something?" We were there all night and I think it was about ten to six when we came out when the all clear went. They allowed us out and they said, "Go up and tidy your benches and you can go home".

York's other big chocolate factory was Terry's, and Winnie Mothers-dale remembers,

> *Hill's from Manchester came and took so much of Terry's over and I was working on aircraft propellers. Six of us went to Manchester to the firm in Trafford to train for this work. Another girl and I did our job, then two more did another stage and then two more did another stage. So when we came back we were there training other girls. Terry's was still working but at a very small capacity. We did shifts at Hill's, and the person coming on the next shift, the next foreman, if he was late I couldn't come away until he turned up, which was a bit unfortunate as he wasn't a very good timekeeper. One of the girls, her brother in law was on the Gold Coast [now Ghana] and he came over on leave and brought some of those little Canary bananas, very small and very sweet, and she gave me two. Ooh, well it was an absolute luxury. I've never known two bananas make so many sandwiches in my life.*

Cissie Colley worked at Terry's during the war.

> *It was underground, there was no windows, and we were painting aeroplane blades. It had to be a certain amount of varnish and if you got more varnish on, you'd to scrape it off. It went through ever so many processes before it was finished. You had to come up to go to the toilet and a girl that I'd worked with all my life as a factory girl, we both went upstairs and we fell asleep on the toilets and we were there when they come to work. We were very, very tired. We'd to go to it next day just the same, seven days a week, and if they wanted you on a Sunday you had to go in. I seem to remember they dropped all the laws about rules and regulations about labour, during the war. There was no Bank Holidays and all that. It was an awful big place, there was quite a number of people who worked in there, but it never ever got hit.*

> *We had firewatching practice, what to do if bombs dropped. You had to keep your cool.*

It was terribly important, doing aeroplane propellers. They were losing a lot of aeroplanes. My Auntie Florrie did shift work, she was on the same shift as me. She were a dear, she was a wonderful old lady, she kept us all alive. When we had our break, she'd dance and sing and act the fool. Everybody was friendly, people were much more friendly in those days.

Three times I got dermatitis right up to my elbow, with the paint you see. The doctor kept giving me cream, he said, "There's nothing you can do about this". When the war finished, the men were coming back, and Mr Smith, the foreman, he didn't want me to finish work. He said, "You can go up to the factory, packing chocolates".

Jack and Keith Turner's father worked on the railway, as Jack recalls.

His job was controller on the railway. Before the war, the offices were in Toft Green, directly across from the railings. When war had broken out, they realised this was essential and they moved. If you go onto the bar walls at Micklegate Bar, and turn towards the Minster, and stand and look across Lendal Bridge, on the left is the present station, on the right

Jack and Keith Turner, 2005
(Van Wilson)

you drop down into the moat. There were some ventilators there, quite high and the control office was under the moat. There was a massive big wall with steel doors and a diesel engine generator, air purifier and everything else. We lived in Scarcroft Road, there was often a knock on the door, "Can you come in, we're one short, can you come in?" It got to such a state that mother said, "No, he's not in". He was in bed trying to get some sleep. 12 hour days were nothing to him. On a Sunday I used to take his dinner to him. She used to plate his dinner, put it in a bag. Then down Queen Street, up the slope, through the little gate and down the steps. Quite a few worked there. There were banks of phones.

Joan Pannett was 20 when the war began. She worked at the York Carriageworks on Holgate Road, where parts were being made for the wings of the Blackburn Botha aircraft.

I was inspecting component parts for the wings. The aircraft were built in Hull. It was huge like a hangar, and both sides were all these gantries with the machinery in, with all wire netting around. There was a lot of men in there, a lot of railway men. I suppose they'd maybe been somewhere and they taught us how to do it. They came out of the railway shops. That was their war effort.

Joan Pannett 2005 (Mike Race)

We started at seven on a morning, then you would have a break for coffee, then you had a lunch break. Then a tea-break in the afternoon and we worked through until eight at night. You did that one week, then you did 8 o'clock to seven next morning when you were on nights. Some of them were out of alignment, that's why you inspected them, to see if they were fit to be put on the wing of the aircraft. But they had inspectors out there on the production as well.

Joan Pannett at York Carriageworks 1944, on third row from front, second from left, next to her twin sister. (Joan Pannett)

We just had a green overall. The women had trousers on for climbing about. They used to weld and everything, they really did a man's job. I don't think women got the same pay as a man, no matter what they were doing.

We used to all go out on a night. All the managers and the foreman, we'd go to Micklegate, to the Queen. Some of the lads used to get over the wall after they'd checked in on a night and go down to t'pub, had a drink at the Fox. They thought we didn't know, but we did, we'd see them creeping back. It was real friendly, it was a real laugh, we enjoyed working there. I played a practical joke when my [twin] sister came. She was sent down to Terry's old factory, she had a real heavy men's job down there, big vats of hot chocolate, and she didn't like it. I asked one of the foremen if there was any chance for her and he said, "Yes, send her, if she's anything like you". So she came. The first morning, I never told anybody she was coming and I took her in and sat her down at a desk and said, "I won't be long, I'm just going to the cloakroom". I was

127

*watching through this crack in the door and I saw Harry Warrington
[who was also a local pianist] come in. I knew what he'd do, 'cos he
used to do it to me every morning. He used to say, "Now then Joan",
and give me a thump on my back. And he did it to her. Well she looked
at him and he looked down at her, and I said, "Are you wanting me?"
And he looked round and he couldn't believe it. They used to get us
mixed up even there. We were really identical. We used to make our
own fun, we were always doing something that we shouldn't have been.
But you'd to do your work.*

*When it was our days off, we always used to ride out to Kirkham Abbey
on our bikes. Two of the girls who were on production, they had a
caravan at Knaresborough and we would cycle there on a weekend and
all stay in this caravan. We'd go in the river swimming, we had the
time of our lives there. Or we'd get a boat out and row up to Bishopthorpe.*

George Wilson worked at Elvington.

*When the aerodrome was first set out, I was the first or second man
to start on it. I was working for a London firm but transferred to the
contractors Walker and Slater from Derby. I had about 12 months
with them as foreman and then I turned over to the Air Ministry as
Assistant Clerk of Works and I stayed there all the war. I was superintendent, maintaining the buildings and runways. We had to do that to
keep the planes up in the air, there were four runways and they couldn't
afford to have one of those vacant when the planes was coming in. It
was an English squadron first [77 Squadron] then the Free French.
There was quite a few planes, and they could set off to go bombing and
three or four failed to return, but the next lunchtime they were replaced.
We had some big losses, sometimes five or six in a night. When they
first started there was no heating in the planes, and they'd come back
frozen stiff. I've seen them when they've been shot up and they still go
back again and you've had to lift the dead out and the frozen ones out of*

the plane. How they landed, I don't know. Some of the planes, you could drive a motor car through the hole that they'd made in the wings.

There'd be a couple of thousand men on the 'drome. We had a few severe accidents. Three or four days after Christmas, the crew had gone on leave and a spare ground staff had been put on to service the plane and load it up with bombs ready for going out, but somebody pulled the wrong cord and the bombs started whistling and exploded and the lot went up. The fire engines were always in readiness and they got there to do what they could. But another bomb went off and they went up with it as well, I think there were 14 killed that day. It'd be Christmas '44. There was one occasion one Sunday night, and one had a thousand pound bomb on him and he couldn't dispose of it coming home and as he hit the runway the bomb went off. It blew him sky high and in the runway there was a massive hole. You could get a double decker bus in it. The Free French were good lads, and the British crews, marvellous. They used to go into York, there was a special bus used to run every night to take the crews in. Some of them never bothered about coming home, the first cycle they came across they used to whip it and bring it right out here, and within a few hundred yards of the entrance to the 'drome, they used to throw it into the hedge bottom. We could go up in a morning and there were cycles scattered about all over. The police was forever here taking cycles away.

I used to be on the 'drome night after night and they never supplied us with a shelter. When they went on these long bombing trips, I got a gang of men out, and there'd been a drop of rain or the runway had a bit of ice, and it had to be sanded and salted ready for them coming in.

We had separate offices and we hadn't a great deal to do with the French but we used to have French lessons once a week. The admin officer, a squadron leader, he was a French racing motorist, and had a big red Honda car, and he asked me if we had a fitter that could get another ten mile an hour out of it. He said he'd give them ten pound if they could.

Then he said, "Come on, Mr Wilson, we'll have a ride in it". And he took it down the runway and he got to 115 miles an hour. I said, "I'll get out this end. I'll be taking off if I go back there with you".

There were other instances of our own planes crashing in the city. Alwyn Banks recalls

I was involved with the Halifax bomber that crashed on Nunthorpe Grove. I was with my electrician on a motorbike and sidecar, and we were just going over Skeldergate Bridge when the plane crashed, and we went straight to Nunthorpe Grove. There were some bombs lying in the road but also a lot of fuel had gone over houses, and the backs of houses were on fire. We were there before the fire brigade so we went down all the houses and drew all the main fuses so that when the firemen came they could put the hoses on without worrying about any electricity. And whilst I was there, a chap called from a house, "Have you got any tools?" I had my leather belt with my hammer and screwdrivers and pliers. One of the crew had come through the roof of his house into the bathroom, and the chap couldn't open the door so I had to go up and knock the door hinges off to get this navigator out. But unfortunately he was dead. One of the crew had bailed out and when the plane crashed, there was an explosion and it blew him back up in the air and his parachute opened and he came down at Southlands Chapel. And there were some Italian prisoners of war there who looked after him until an ambulance came. I think he was the only survivor.

Brothers Jack and Keith Turner were living in Scarcroft Road. Jack recalls,

There was a massive water tank on Scarcroft Green, for putting out fires. On the green you can just see the line of an air raid shelter under-ground. Near the railings of the school, the shelters were above ground. We certainly remember the plane that came down on Nunthorpe Grove. It was so loud, I thought it was scraping the roof. We were stood on

Southlands Road looking down as it was burning away. Somebody said, "Get under, the tank's going to go up", and we dived under an ambulance.

Keith remembers,

We were beaten there by soldiers in Park Street, 'cos that was requisitioned for soldiers and they hopped over the end and across the bowling green. They used to use Scarcroft for training, the army requisitioned places to train troops.

COOKE, TROUGHTON AND SIMS

Many people recall this firm, which became Vickers Instruments in the 1960s. Bob Ferguson worked at Cooke's.

It was widely known before the war as an optical instrument factory all over the country. During the war we had to transfer our production over from optical instruments like microscopes, to tank periscopes, predictor telescopes, instruments that were useful to the war effort.

Joan Sadler worked for the company.

When your call-up papers came when you were 20, you filled in this form, if you wanted to go into the services, or munitions. At Cooke's, we worked in a department where you inspected the components before they went onto final assembly lines. Screws, bolts, nuts, figure components.

It was a vast change after being in a factory and working with women. It was mixed. It gave you a new outlook on life. It makes it a bit more interesting if you've got men there as well. I think the war changed so many things. I think it gave people a lot more freedom.

Peter Goater recalls

At Cooke's we made sighting telescopes, they all had a number, and a 32 sighting telescope was one that you clamped on a rifle. They were nearly all exported. There was the siege of Stalingrad and we made these 2000 telescopes, not for Russian men, but for Russian women. Women were snipers, they were brilliant with a rifle. I only found out they were going there 'cos I happened to be in our export office at the time. You made a bigger one, a 53, which went outside of the artillery. We made a star shell case used by bomb aimers. They were sighted through this case.

We made theodolites, used this spider's web. You got the spider from Strensall Common. You went with little boxes. It's a special spider with a speckled back, they put it on a fork and wrapped its web, so you wind the fork up and you put it over the braticule and glue it. Why they use a spider's web is because you can go to the Arctic, and to Africa and it won't alter. If you use metal, it starts bending 'cos it can't stand heat or cold. A web can stand the heat and cold. It has to be in its own environment, which was Strensall Common, to be built up. It gave a perfect web. Captain Scott used one of Cooke's theodolites, it's in the Science Museum and the web is still good.

Kate Houghton began work in 1943. She was nearly 17.

I first went to work at the Post Office, and Telegraphs was behind the counter. We talked a lot to Elvington aerodrome. We'd maybe converse a bit with them on the phone, and send all their telegrams in French. [The Free French Air Force was based there later in the war]. *We were able to give them a bit of joy, a bit of a laugh. Where the Leather Shop is now in Lendal, the messenger boys came down that passage into a room which was attached to our telegraph room, which was full of teleprinters where we all sat. We had earphones and mouthpieces. Or we would be sitting at teleprinters with screens of tape with 'Regret to*

Kate Houghton 2004
(Kate Houghton)

Kate Houghton in 1940s
(Kate Houghton)

inform you' telegrams and things like that. The messenger boys would
come into this extra room with a glass window and a shutter and
then when telegrams went through, this was open. My hours could be
anything between 7.30 in the morning and we finished at 9.17 at night.
I loved it. We were doing our bit, I suppose, for the war effort. We used
to do split duties as well. Sometimes we could take time off and go to
the cinema so that was good. We used to have a packed lunch, or we
had meals we could put in the oven, like meat and potato pie. And then
there was Bettys, and another café in Lendal, Miss Welch's. That was
very nice.

We were very busy all the time because in those days the way that
people got news was through telegrams. They would go into yellow
envelopes and away they would go. Most of us had the horrible task of

taking the tape, you suddenly realised that you were taking the letter to the parents to say they'd either been killed in action or they were a prisoner of war. So one or two of the staff went out of the room in tears.

There were messages coming from overseas. We were on the phone to various people at Leeds who would pass on a lot of messages. We used to talk in the language that kids are using now, [in text messages], like 'RU OK'. And tonight was always 'tonite', and 'Tks' for thanks. So nothing's new. We had a shorthand for getting through to other post offices. We worked to all the RAF stations around. We were sworn to secrecy in the Post Office, we signed the pledge. We saw some telegrams that we used to get for the RAF station. We didn't really know, we just did our job.

1944, when I was 17, it was one of the best years of my life. I had a lovely Canadian boyfriend, we had a wonderful time, dancing, innocent fun but lovely. And we worked in such an exciting spot in a way. It was one of the best years. And I imagine my friends would agree.

Mary Beilby worked as a matron at Newburgh Priory but then moved to York when she was married. She mentioned that the war took away her young life, she 'didn't really have a twenties'.

I worked at the Ministry of Labour, down Piccadilly next to the tax office. You got called up and if you were married, they couldn't send you away but if you'd no children you had to work full-time. If you were single, you were mobile and had a choice of the forces, ammunitions, and Land Army. They'd called up all the original permanent staff, so they were relying on married women. They were mostly married women that could work full-time, and we used to work alternate Saturday afternoons registering all the women that used to come in. They'd start perhaps with 19 year olds, and then it would be the next age and then the next age. At the end of the war they'd got well into the 40s I think.

Mary Beilby 2005
(Van Wilson)

Mary and Robert Beilby on their
wedding day
(Mary Beilby)

*We used to send women to Handley Page factory, [based at the aero-
drome in Clifton]. And they used to sit in the fuselage of these Halifaxes that they were repairing and knit in the night-time. They didn't
know what to give them to do 'cos they hadn't trained them. There
were a lot that didn't pull their weight, but it maybe wasn't their fault
because you had to draft them somewhere.*

Of course a lot of the women qualified as riveters, and worked at
patching the shell holes on the fuselage.

Una Hiscoe 2005 (Una Hiscoe)

Una Hiscoe as young woman
(Una Hiscoe)

Una Hiscoe began to work for Handley Page, in about 1943, involved
in the finances of the canteen.

*First I worked for Ryvita. A London firm who were bombed out and
they came to York then they moved down to Leicester. Nobody believes
me but they did have a chocolate Ryvita but it can't have been a success
or it would have gone into production. Rowntree's did a lot of work
for them. I moved to Leicester with them then I came back to York.
That was when I was working up on the drome. It was a repair depot,
they didn't build the Halifaxes there. They came in for repairs. They
were like great big hangars where the aircraft went. And it was mostly
women working in the hangars.*

*Everybody was directed into work, you couldn't just go where you
wanted, it was where you were sent. I went down to the Labour
Exchange, and they sent me up there. I was working in the office. Just
general, to do with money, the paperwork. The chief test pilot wouldn't
eat with the gang. So he always came to my office for his meals. I used*

to cycle all the way, from Acomb to Clifton [before Clifton Bridge was built], *and we had at lunchtimes 'Music while you Work'. I had to more or less supervise. We did them a breakfast, and lunches, and I think we did them a tea-break. And then they had a meal at night as well before I came away. I think there was about 40 staff in the canteen.*

Mary Beilby's husband, Robert, worked there, as their son Nick recalls,

He was a fitter, at what is now Clifton Moor, and he worked on hydraulics and pneumatics. He worked on the control systems to the Halifaxes, basically putting the pipework together that enabled the pilot to control the aircraft through hydraulic air systems. It was quite an involved job. He worked lots of hours, and shifts. It was Handley Page that owned the factory, they were from Cricklewood in London. They had other factories.

I think it was something he'd always wanted to do. He was passionate about his aircraft. He'd certainly worked a bit on civil engineering in the York area on water schemes, and on the Derwent. I think when the war came along, he retrained. He wanted to join the RAF but he had polio as a child and he tried several times, but they turned him down. So he did the next best thing, he worked on aircraft. But he had to go and train and learn the engineering skills. But he loved the work and he also had lots of laughs. It'd be seen as very politically incorrect now but I think it's funny anyway, some of the jokes they played on the women. Getting them to file rubber and go looking for left-handed screwdrivers.

My father recalled he went to work one morning and there'd been a bombing raid and one of the hangars had been hit and was as flat as a pancake. I do recall him saying that some of the aircraft that came back for repair, were in a heck of a mess. It was rather a gruesome job for those who were working on them 'cos clearly they'd not been cleaned out, and there were human remains and all sorts in some of them. But he didn't talk about that side too much. He used to make light of it and tell the jokey side of life, but I think it was grim at times.

They used to dismantle them and take the wings off and put them on long low loaders, lorries, a thing that they called Queen Mary's. And they could take the fuselage from the airfield, and straight into Handley Page, where they could either dismantle them for spares or repair them and put them back into airworthy condition.

People were working on it, 24 hours a day, seven days a week. And the production rates I suspect as the war went on, got better and better. They closed the Handley Page factory in York at the end of war, and they scrapped old Halifaxes. I heard my father say there were just rows and rows of Halifaxes waiting to be scrapped. He found that quite sad really, that there was no further use for them. He used to say to me, that when he retired, he'd love to work on a Halifax again, and of course there wasn't one. And I think within probably a couple of years of him dying, the Halifax project started. So I think it would have been ideal for him, he could have gone to Elvington and worked on a Halifax again.

Nick is referring to the project at the Elvington air museum to rebuild a Halifax aircraft, something which has been realised, although the aircraft does not fly.

They'd done their job and the technology had moved on. There wasn't the need for that amount of heavy bombers. And when they did retain heavy bombers, they retained some Lancasters after the war for further usage. The Halifaxes had done their job, they'd done their time and there was nothing really they could do. And of course they were moving into the jet age so really they were history.

Eileen Brown was the first woman driver at York Station. Before the war, far fewer women actually drove, but that changed during the six years of war.

Eileen Brown, 1930s (Eileen Brown)

I was a porter on the platform. There was no signs to tell you where anything was going, on account of if an invasion came. So we all had to know exactly which train was going where. Trains used to come in with wounded soldiers, and they were all shouting to you and you were getting them teas and all that. Keeping 'em all happy. There used to be hardly any lights in those days. Every light was shielded. Then I found a lady's fur coat, she'd left it on a train. And the stationmaster asked me if I would like anything [as a reward] and I said, "If ever there's any women drivers, yes", and I would be the first woman driver at York, because they taught me to drive.

I was with a man about two days, and then they give me an old van and I was in the goods yard, and I come on every morning and drove round that yard for a week, reversing and whatever, then coming out into the city with all the cars. Then I was driving railway vans and parcel wagons. I loved it, a hard job but nice. You were out in the open air. And when they bombed York, they bombed right over the railway, and next morning we had to go to work to our vans, I think there was two girls driving then. I went and got on me van and they said, "Stay there, because you'll have something to do". No work because everything was bombed. And they put a bag in the back of me van and a policeman come to sit at side of me and he said, "You're going to Kent Street, love". He says, "You don't know what's in the bag?" I said, "No". Well it was the body of a man who was killed and I took his body to the mortuary in Kent Street, which was the old cattle market. And the policeman said to me, "Don't come in and look". But my curiosity overcame me and I did go in and all the bodies were laid out, families, mothers and fathers and children.

Christine Rayson left school in 1940 at the age of sixteen. She began with voluntary work,

at the Military Hospital, on Fulford Road opposite the barracks. I worked for an orthopaedic specialist, taking his notes, going from bed to bed, on his patients. It was Dickie Metcalfe whose uncle was Dr Hood at York. They were getting ready for going out to the desert, combining getting equipment in and staff in to send out to the western desert. I was on the secretarial side. Just previous to that, I went and worked at the NAAFI canteen there.

Christine Rayson (centre) with Esther Lee (left) and Arlene Kemp (right) and Canadian officers in Stonegate (Christine Rayson)
Christine Rayson 2005 (Van Wilson)

Christine then got a job at the

Canadian Knights of Columbus in Stonegate. We worked with the Canadian Air Force, 6 Group who were stationed at Allerton Park, the headquarters. I did work on the various dromes, working alongside the Canadian YMCA. The head office was in London. The Canadian army also came up. They were stationed around Helmsley.

It's a Roman Catholic organisation actually, the Knights of Columbus, and the Monseigneur in charge of the Roman Catholic chaplains in England came to visit us, and was very shocked to find we were all Church of England. The Canadian government was a very good government, a very generous government to their troops, looked after them very well. Whatever the forces wanted had to be supplied, hospitality, hotels, sending cables, ordering whatever they wanted from back home. We had to deal with them through Western Cable Company. They wanted everything that you could imagine. Even sorting out the children. I sent a honeymoon couple to Scarborough, and the baby was born on the honeymoon with no children's clothes or anything, everything was on coupons. I got a very irate boarding housekeeper from Scarborough on my tail. She'd had all the backwash of it.

They'd come in to talk to us. They seemed to sense if something was going to happen to them, it was very, very odd. They didn't think they were going to come back, and a lot of them didn't. But it was a sort of foreboding that they had. They used to be sort of not with you and yet they wanted to talk to you. You always knew when there were going to be bombing raids because ringing the dromes, we couldn't get through to them. It was always, "Calls are not being accepted". I worked there until about 1946. The original staff were English and then two Canadian girls came in and joined us. I went to all the dromes, Linton, East Moor, Tholthorpe, Middleton St George, Skipton.

The place in Stonegate, it's a shop, and our offices actually were above. It was almost opposite Little Stonegate. And on the top floor was the ironing room. That was another of the facilities. One of them nearly burned us down actually. He left the iron on the floor switched on, and a fire started. And we were accused of trying to set the whole of Stonegate on fire. We had all the fire brigade because it's a' red area', 'cos it's so medieval and they're so old, the properties. Well all the wood flooring had to come up, and cork was put down, and it was quite a mess. So all the fire brigade arrived and ordered us out of the building and started to dig up the floorboards to try and stop the smoke that was coming out.

Evelyn Hudson wearing Observer Corps uniform, 1943 (Evelyn Hudson)

Evelyn Hudson 2005 (Mike Race)

Evelyn Hudson started work at Kathleen Benson's hairdressers in York but in 1943,

I badly burned my hand and so of course I couldn't do any actual hairdressing and Kathleen Benson put me on the reception desk, which I enjoyed. But then I volunteered for the Observer Corps, partly so

that I could stay at home with my mum and my sister. They were fairly happy times, they were a good set of girls, and we had some rare old fun. One of the girls, Hazel, lived at Whitby, but she stayed in York all week in lodgings. If we came off nights on Friday morning, 8 o'clock, we weren't on again till 8 o'clock Monday morning, and there used to be four of us go with Hazel to her home at Whitby, and it was all barbed wire and sandbags but we still went dancing to the Spa and we used to have some hectic weekends.

The Observer Corps was on Knavesmire. York 9 and York 10. It covered a fair area of Yorkshire and just into Lincolnshire. The table top was thick rubber with a map of all the airfields. You all had your own position round the table and four airfields you were in touch with, with the men in the field. Counting the planes going and counting them coming back. "I've got two missing", or, "I've got three missing". The officers were on a balcony round the top. Then about six in the morning, they would come through and say, "Had a phone call from Sussex (or Surrey or Suffolk), two planes have landed". Thank goodness! If they were

York Observer Corps 1943, Evelyn Hudson is on back row, second from left
(Evelyn Hudson)

disarmed, disabled, they used to land on the airfields in the south of England. And you used to get to know the voices. You probably never met the men but you knew the voices. They were very brave, those fellows, 'cos they were just stood in the middle of a field with a tin hat on.

We used to have some fun as well. We had one girl and she was lovely and so helpful. And I can remember she rang upstairs (you could press your button and ring to the officers if you had a query), and she said, "Got so-and-so airfield on the phone, plane lights at north-north-west, travelling at such and such a speed", (which they used to give you), "and he says it sounds like a glider." Well it went on the tannoy, and everybody just cracked, and then she suddenly realised, she said, "Wait while I get my hands on him!" They used to do bits of teasing, if it was a quiet night. We didn't have many quiet nights but we were supposed to have an hour's break where you could get something to eat or put your head down. But more than one night we didn't get the chance, especially when they started the thousand bomber raids from the airfields in Yorkshire. And of course York was a focal point. They used to take off and circle till every plane was in the air and then they went either south or the North Sea.

Sometimes we got a break because there was quite a number of male and female volunteers. They used to come on at four in the afternoon till eight, so that they could spell [take over from] any girl that wanted a relief or wasn't very well. You were sat there with your earphones on and until you got relieved you couldn't take your earphones off. I mean we got daylight raids. When I first started, there was a lot of planes took off, in daylight, dropping leaflets. They all had to be monitored there and back. You plotted them while they were in your area and then you passed them over to the next area. It was all on the one table. It went from Newcastle to somewhere in Cumbria, Birkenhead, Derbyshire, Lincolnshire and all the Yorkshire coast.

The big raids were a bit tense at times. We only knew either that they

Observer Corps personnel plotting aircraft – reconstruction from Eden Camp museum. (Christine Kyriacou)

were going south, south-west, south-east, I mean the airmen themselves didn't always know until they got in the air. We used to meet quite a few of them because they'd invite us to their dances at Tholthorpe, Holme-on-Spalding-Moor, East Moor, Linton. They would send a wagon for us. Everybody just lived for the day, you didn't know what was going to happen next day.

And then there was a big map up on the wall. The girls had to go up ladders, and that was for the coastline to Newcastle and the North Sea, and we always had a plane about five o'clock in the morning, which we used to call Weather Willie. He was a German who used to come obviously sussing out the weather. Didn't do anything much, but you had to plot him. It was a bit boring being up at that, because there wasn't much doing. It was better when you were on the table.

The radar stations, I suppose they were secret really, but that was why they had to have so many points for massing together before they set off, so the radar could keep their eye on them. Our table plotted them from *take-off to the air and then they were passed on actually to the Air Force and they tracked them on the radar screen. When the bombers were coming back, which could be any time from four till seven, it depended how far they'd been, they used to be very keen, because the Germans sometimes used to run under them and come back in their area, and bomb their airfields before they could land. So the outside crews had to be very keen with their spotting to spot these other planes, 'cos they did sneak in.*

The crews were in, like a little brick, or sometimes only straw and earth, little shelter with a theodolite thing which tracked, and they just said, "North-north-east", and whichever way he was going and what height he was going. The fellows in the fields were spot on, and they were all volunteers, they weren't paid. A lot of them were farmers and shift men, from the shipyards, and from the railways. They'd get up and go out and do a four hour stint in the middle of the night. A lot of the officers were volunteers. There was Scott Marr, who was a designer at Terry's, designed the chocolate boxes, and Harry Shouksmith, Shouksmith's Plumbers, he was another officer.

I can remember D-Day morning. We'd had umpteen thousand bomber raids, and this particular night, the lines were buzzing and everybody was busy. I'd got 60, 70, 80, 100, you know, in different areas, and the rumour went round, "Oh, something big's happening, they'll be going to Berlin," which was a guess really. And we never got a break that night, we were at it all night, and then about half past four, the bell went which came from above which meant, "Everybody quiet!" We used to get that if there was a raid in York, but this particular time everybody stopped and then Eisenhower's voice came over, "We are pleased to announce that British, Canadian and American troops have landed in France, in Normandy."

It was great. I came home, I'd make a cup of tea, take me mum a cup of tea to bed and then she got up, and she would bring me some breakfast after I'd had a bath or a wash. I can remember going in and slamming the front door, going up stairs, knocking on my mother's bedroom door and I said, "It's D-Day," and with that I was in bed and absolutely hard asleep. Then my mother woke me about three o'clock, and she says, "You were right, it is."

Mildred Veal was born in Hull in 1922. Her parents moved to York where she has lived since the war, but her role during the war was as a gunner with the ATS.

Mildred Veal as a gunner at Oswestry (Mildred Veal)

Mildred Veal in 1990s (Mildred Veal)

I can remember that my Dad had one of the real old Fords and he took me to Hull station. From Hull station to Durham and Durham was the place you got the training. From there I went to a gunner place, but I was just an ordinary clerk with 5th North Staffs regiment. Then they asked for volunteers for ack ack so I went. It was the 30th of December 1941.

I was with a searchlight battery which was all men, there was only about eight girls there. And I was a clerk in the Quartermaster's stores. Then I would be at Owestry for a long while because it was radar, well, GL it was called in those days. You had to have a longer teaching before we went out to go on to the gun sites. All that was secret.

There was an engine that we 8 stone 8ers had to turn and it was a 15,000 volt generator. Then there was a transmitter which sent up the things to the aeroplane. Then the receiver which is when you came down and found them on these little televisions. You've got like a caravan and there were four of us in there. Then one, the bossy one, was giving the information through onto the gun park and we had a transmitter. And then there was this generator which stank of oil. The girls didn't fire the guns, the men did. Even the things that went in [shells] were very heavy. They were older men, the men that were in their forties who weren't strong enough to be going out and doing what the youngsters were doing.

I suppose we weren't frightened, you never thought about it. Yes it was a hard thing to do and when there was guns going up, but you were doing your work, you'd got to get on with it and that was it. As my mother would say, "You gird your loins, you have a cup of tea, you do whatever you've got to do and you get on with it"'

We wore boots, and gaiters, trousers, a shirt and tie, a hat, and a leather jacket because it got cold. We couldn't wear a tin hat, with all this equipment that we had. But all the girls on the other parts of the gun site, they wore tin hats. There were some who were more an open target than we were, on the actual gun site.

There were some that were killed. I mean a gun site with eight big guns on it, the Germans would see it. And then the buzz bombs were nasty things, and the other ones where you didn't see them coming until you were dead, there was nothing we could do with those.

I once told a Brigadier to get out. Well, I didn't know he was one. It's very rarely I swear, because my mother would have killed me. There would be four of us on there, all in the dark with these little tiny radar things, on the screen. And somebody opened the door and I just shouted out, "'Shut the bloody door". 'Cos we'd all lost our sight. It was a Brigadier!

We gunners are a different set of people. We are closer to each other than you will find anywhere else. A mate in the army is a mucker. And a mucker will look after you from front, back, top, bottom, sideways and everything. We looked after one another. You imagine a gun site with eight big guns, and everybody there, we were all mates. I mean when you think it's not only the people that went to war. There were the mums at home who must've had a pretty hard life, nurses, doctors, people who made munitions. And the grandmas knitting like fury and helping mothers, everybody helped each other.

Edna Hall married her husband Bill in 1936 and had two children, Robert and Wendy. He had been a teacher before joining the army and was posted to York. They only stayed in York for a year before he was posted on again. Although a lot of women took on work during the war, there were many who could not work and who spent the war keeping the children and the home safe. Their role was less glamorous but important, to keep life going on for their husbands and sweethearts to return to.

Edna and Bill Hall on their wedding day (Edna Hall)

Edna Hall and her son Robert, 2005 (Van Wilson)

I spent my time keeping the children happy and never thought about the war much. All I did was take the children out to the park and the shops. The lady we stayed with was nice. She was one of the fire watchers, and on a Tuesday night she used to do this. Wendy was one of these children who woke at midnight every night and she didn't want to go to sleep again. She almost began to fall asleep just as Robert woke up. This lady used to treat that night as a wash night if she wasn't called out. She used to do her washing in the kitchen and she'd have Wendy sitting in the pram, so that was one night I got a bit of rest.

Robert Hall talks about his father, who was involved in work at the Military Hospital before joining the Army Education Corps.

When they discovered he had a science degree, they made him laboratory assistant and post-mortem attendant at the Military Hospital. One thing they used to do was protect the army from infection of foodstuffs. They had to investigate the purity and bacteriological sterileness of

*bully beef, it was going in large 7lb tins. Not unnaturally he and the
other man in the same post, used to find it necessary to condemn a 7lb
tin every now and then, which would allow it to be used for human
consumption.*

*One event that impressed him a lot was M & B tablets, May and Baker,
I imagine the first manufacturers of sulphanamides in this country,
which before penicillin were the only real antiseptic around. I can
remember having M & B tablets myself when we lived in Sutton Cold-
field when I must have had tonsillitis. You crushed the tablet and took
it on a spoon with jam. You had to drink a lot of extra water because the
end product of the metabolism of the M & B tablet was excreted in the
urine where it tended to crystallise in the kidneys unless the urine was
made particularly dilute by taking in extra liquid. M & B was also used
in the treatment of venereal infection. One of the drivers for the medical
corps attached to the hospital had exposed himself to this risk and
because of his position, driving around medical supplies, he was able
to annexe some M & B tablets.. But not being particularly knowledge-
able, I imagine he thought the more he took, the more likely he would
be cured. He didn't really know about the danger of crystal urea, so he
died of an overdose of M & B tablets. The post-mortem exam, which my
father must have assisted at or attended, was done in the hospital and
the man's kidneys were full of crystal.*

One occupation which was affected in a different way during the
war, was the medical profession. In 1940, GPs reported fewer patients
coming to the surgery, and a drop in home visits. People were 'too busy
to be ill'. There was also a lot of self-help. The press was full of advertisements for products such as Ovaltine 'to alleviate tiredness', Black
Beer and Superior Tarragona Wine 'for nerves, anaemia and sleepless-
ness', Wincarnis Tonic 'to fight against heavy wartime odds', and Phyl-
losan 'to revitalise and rejuvenate'. There were also Milk of Magnesia,
which promised you could, 'in spite of war, enjoy springtime vigour',
and allow you to 'shake off that tired low-spirited feeling', Fynnons

Salts for 'new vigour for the kidneys and liver', Carters Little Liver Pills and Beecham's Pills 'to feel much younger, livelier and happier'. Men over 40 were urged to take Oystrax tablets for 'new life, pep and youth overnight'.

Joan Sadler explains how war affected the working lives of both men and women.

Housewives were going out to work, instead of being tied to their homes. People had little romances. Or if they were young and fancy free, they thought there's an opportunity to get out of a rut of a job they weren't particularly happy in. Fellows who were in mundane jobs that had ability and that got up in the ranks, made a new life for themselves. Everything was much more active, York was a busy place with service people. Women felt a lot more liberated. It changed women's attitudes a lot. Some women were sick with worry, especially married women who had young children, and they were bringing them up entirely on their own without their father. Some men were abroad for five or six years and some men never left the shores, it's just the luck of the draw.

People got really patriotic at the time. There was a camaraderie that never existed before, a tremendous feeling of goodwill and there was always somebody to help out with somebody that had had bad news. We were always writing letters, this is one of the things that fellas said kept them going during the war, letters from home. People were depressed by war, especially people whose boyfriends had gone. It must have been a terrible time to live through if you were madly in love with somebody. I had one cousin whose husband was killed on the beaches of North Africa and she was left with two young children. She's a person I admire tremendously, she brought up those two children on her own. I suppose if you're forced into something, it's amazing what strength you find.

CHAPTER EIGHT
ENTERTAINMENT AND ROMANCE

It is hard to imagine now what life was like before the advent of television, computers, DVD players and mobile phones, but the war generation had no problem in making their own entertainment. Fewer books were being produced due to the shortage of paper, but libraries still operated, although the choice was depleted. Families tended to do things together, like play cards, dominoes or chess, or even make clipped rugs. Friends enjoyed spending time taking long walks and in the summer playing tennis or badminton in their leisure time. Of course people worked long hours and many did voluntary war work in their spare time. But entertainment was important, because it helped people to forget the war, at least for a time, and put aside their anxieties and fears.

Avril Appleton recalls how families made their own entertainment.

We had rabbit pie suppers at friends' houses and we all did a turn. My brother wrote little plays and we all got dressed up. My mother used to recite 'There's a little yellow idol to the north of Kathmandu'.

The radio played an important part, with families often gathering round to listen to a wide range of programmes. ITMA, which stands for 'It's That Man Again', was a regular 'sitcom' and incredibly popular. It featured Tommy Handley and others playing characters which satirised the war. Mabel Robson enjoyed listening, and on Saturday nights, her friend would come over, and once her daughter went to bed,

We would sit knitting and listening to the radio to all the murders and things. I'm sure there wasn't enough, we used to be knitting that fast. And ITMA, they used to say, "Dis is Funf speaking", and "Can I do you now sir?"

There were also concerts broadcast, with classical music and
dance bands, as Walter Davy
recalls.

*As a child, during the war, it
was when all the American and
Canadian servicemen were over
here, the Glenn Miller style, big
bands, that's when I first got
interested in it. What I heard, I
liked, it was as simple as that, the*

Walter Davy in 1950s (Walter Davy)

*quality and the talents of the musicians. I was a big Artie Shaw fan,
Benny Goodman very much so, and the drumming of Gene Krupa. I
was brought up on this, and I have obviously very nostalgic thoughts of
the war.*

Peter Binns, who relates the story of losing his home during the
Baedeker Raid, in the chapter on 'Air Raids', went on to work for many
years for York Radio Relay.

*On 1st September 1939, the BBC brought out the single Home Service
on radio (then called the wireless). This included all the government's
news and public service announcements. Radio was important in
wartime partly because it was the vehicle for government announcements but also because it provided music, both popular and serious,
drama and comedy, allowing people the opportunity to escape for
a while from the war. In January 1940 there was also a Forces
Programme.*

Radio Luxemburg had been very popular from the 30s onwards, [it
began broadcasting in 1933], *and was again after the war, but went
off the air along with other commercial stations on the continent when
Hitler invaded these countries.*

York Radio Relay was based in Parliament Street, with operations coming from the basement, which was reinforced by baulks of timber to support the ceiling. The system serviced the Civil Defence. The warning system had its bell in Parliament Street which would sound when the alarm came from the Guildhall. The building had its own generator in case of power cuts. An old Morris car engine was installed in the basement, which was attached to a 240 volt generator. If the German aircraft were approaching this area, the local BBC transmitters went off the air to prevent signals being used as homing devices by the enemy. Parliament Street bunker was also used by fire watchers who were there every night, often playing long games of chess. There was also a Hessian sack and a hammer. Orders were, that if a German invasion took place, the sack would be put over the main amps and the hammer used to smash them. Some of the staff joined the Home Guard.

People certainly bought fewer books during the war, as far fewer were printed. But one publisher, Penguin Books, which was established by Allen Lane in the 1930s, continued to produce popular paperbacks. And this was not just for those on the home front. Pickering's of High Ousegate advertised in the *Yorkshire Evening Press* in April 1940,

'Those serving abroad eagerly welcome books. We have a large stock of sixpenny Penguins and other cheap editions. Just the thing to send them'.

A soldier with the British Expeditionary Force, in France, wrote to the *Yorkshire Evening Press* asking if anyone could provide a gramophone and some records for him and his comrades. Almost immediately 14 gramophones were handed in. One was sent off to his troop and others donated to groups of soldiers in this country on isolated sites. Troops in York asked for a selection of paperback thrillers including Edgar Wallace and Leslie Charteris, adventure novels and Wild West stories. In five days, the public had donated 600 paperbacks.

As well as the radio, live music was much enjoyed. This was sometimes in the form of concerts. In October 1939 a weekly series of concerts for the troops was held in Melbourne Chapel schoolrooms.

Bert Keech Band at De Grey Rooms for radio broadcast, 1944. (York Oral History Society)

Dancing was one of the major forms of entertainment in the 1940s. There were many dance bands in York, with many different venues, so that one could go dancing every night.

In one week in January 1943, for example, it was possible to see the Ambassadors Dance Band at the Albany in Goodramgate, for 1/6d, Bert Keech and his Band at the De Grey Rooms for 2/6d, and Derek Dunning and his Band at the Clifton Ballroom for 1/6d, as well as dances at Terry's Ballroom and the Co-op Hall. Or, as an alternative, there were tea dances at Clifton Cinema. The blackout lasted from

5.28pm to 8.53am. In summer, of course, the country was on double summer time, which meant that clocks went forward two hours instead of one and it did not get dark until almost midnight.

Sheila White was very keen on dancing. She worked at Rowntree's, and,

> *They used to put records on and we'd dance, lunchtimes and evenings. You'd pay a penny and it went to the Red Cross. Sometimes on a Saturday night it was 6d to see Derek Dunning and his Band. A lot of musicians started out at Rowntree's.*

Sheila White dancing at De Grey Rooms, 1943 (Sheila White)

Sheila White, 2005 (Van Wilson)

Alwyn Banks recalls,

Pat [his wife] and I both liked dancing, I used to go a lot to the De Grey Rooms, the Co-op and the English Martyrs by the side of the Odeon. A friend of mine played in a little quartet, the pianist Bob Hirst, and he and I went to school together. His father was a policeman and he ran the police canteen at Clifford Street and they lived in the flat above the fire station. The Albany, that had a sprung floor and that was very nice. Bert Keech at the De Grey Rooms really was my favourite. We used to go out in a crowd, laughing and talking and walking home late at night. At New Year we went to Terry's near the Mansion House. That was beautiful, probably the best in York, with the restaurant and the dance floor up above. Occasionally we went to the nurses' dance at Naburn. We had to cycle out there on a Saturday night, it was jolly nice. They put on a buffet as well. Then cycle home by moonlight. Bobby Hirst also played the piano accordion, played round the pubs at night when he was a schoolboy and he was late for school many times. He was very gifted. For a time he played in the Cantonese restaurant in Coney Street, the Willow. That's where we used to go on a Sunday morning and have coffee and digestive biscuits.

Dancing was something that the young people really looked forward to and were able to lose themselves in for a while. We had lots of air force people around York who came into the dances, particularly the Canadians from East Moor and the French from Elvington. The Canadians tended to go a lot to the Co-op. They were happy times and everybody enjoyed themselves and made the best of it. We made lots and lots of friends, which we still have, we still see people from those days.

Joan Sadler remembers,

We belonged to the Young Women's Christian Association as youngsters, and they had different classes on different evenings of the week, and one hour on a Wednesday night after a keep fit thing was learning

*Joan Sadler during the war
(Joan Sadler) and Joan Sadler
2007 (Van Wilson)*

to dance. Waltzes and foxtrots and the big band sound.

*At the beginning of the war, there was a ban on troops coming within
a six mile radius of York. It was all due to security at that time, so
that meant that Strensall Barracks, they couldn't come into York, only
on special passes. The Archbishop, William Temple, his wife was in
charge of the YMCA canteen for Strensall, and she wrote to personnel
at Rowntree's, to see if they could organise parties of girls to go on a
Saturday night and dance in the canteen with the soldiers. You were
selected to go in the coach that was provided by a chaperone, an older
person looking after the whole bus load. When they said the bus was*

leaving at half past ten, you didn't have to be missing at half ten. No alcohol, not in the YMCA canteen, there was tea and coffee. I think we were reasonably good dancers so we had a good time.

During the course of the Saturday evening dances we would probably be invited along to dances during the week, and we used to cycle out to Strensall. We didn't seem to have many dresses. My mother was a widow and we didn't have much money to spare. We had no chance to save any money. In those days the cycles had dress guards so that your dresses didn't get caught. It really was a fun time. I look back on it with such happiness. It was proper dancing, and in those days those were often the only times someone held you close.

At Strensall they had a marvellous band and a lovely orchestra, and then on Sundays they would have cricket matches. Christmas was such a busy time for dances and parties, you didn't know whether you were coming or going. When the war ended, we wondered how on earth we were going to fill in our time.

And we had the radio. 'Worker's Playtime' was a potpourri of different entertainers, individual artists, and 'Band Wagon' was a two man thing with Arthur Askey and Richard Murdoch. They got into varying situations in everyday life.

Doreen Angus, who was in the Land Army, recalls cycling in to York to the dances.

There was a little shop in Petergate round the back of Dean Court, for about threepence, you wheeled your bicycle down and they kept it in a little place at the back. After the dance we were able to cycle back to Acaster Malbis, without any lights, just a little slit in. We'd always rush to the De Grey Rooms, wait for the Linton bus to arrive with all the airmen and then have a jolly time at the dance. They all came there, those that weren't on flying duties. You could tell 'cos if the bus wasn't

*very full and the ones you hoped to see wouldn't be there, you'd realise
there was obviously a raid going on that night.*

Mary Beilby was married when war began. She recalls meeting her
husband in town after work at the Ministry of Labour.

*We used to work alternate Saturday afternoons registering all the
women that'd come in. [He] used to meet me and we'd go to Bettys for
tea. There was nothing elaborate but mushrooms on toast and tea and
scones. There was a lot of dancing at the City Arms, down the bottom
of Piccadilly. They used to have dancing in High Ousegate, above some
shops there. My husband liked dancing. There wasn't much else to do.*

Joan Pannett worked at the Carriageworks during the war. Like her
colleagues, she worked hard, and so they looked forward to enjoying
their time off.

*We were all going to a dance one night at Stamford Bridge, and one of
the women wanted her hair doing. Of course we were at work so we took
her up on t'gantry. We washed her hair and whipped rollers in. They
had great big lights, they were low and they were real hot, we sat her
down and put her under it and combed it out, she was all ready to go in
t'finish. And we kept looking each way to see if anybody was coming up
them stairs and we left them all guarding us downstairs. We managed
it. Prim they called her, Primrose. We had some really good times.*

Charles Hutchinson was born in Stillington near York. He became a
pianist in a dance band which played in the area from the 1940s.

*I actually started at the village hall at Sutton on the Forest, every
Saturday night. It was a favourite of the Canadian airmen who were at
East Moor. That was the start of my dance band career. I used to have
to ask some of the girls that were dancing at the time, whether I was
playing fast enough, or whether it was fitting right. They were very*

161

helpful, they didn't know anything about music, but they knew whether they could get the steps in or not. You knew if it was a waltz it had to be three four time, and military twosteps had to be six eight time. Quicksteps and foxtrots you learnt from the wireless. Glenn Miller was one, if he was playing something slow, you said, "That would make a slow foxtrot". You never got any real crime because the lads, the Canadians, were glad to be having a night off the camp.

Eddie Lamb worked in the Aeronautical Inspection Department at Cooke, Troughton and Sims. He also played the drums and sang with the Ambassadors dance band.

I used to go to dances at the Albany and during the interval when the band took a break, I would play. Eventually the drummer left and they asked me if I would like to go and I stayed 15 years. Charles Atkinson, who bought the Albany in 1942, said he inherited a dance hall, all the crockery for the cafe and a drummer.

The Ambassadors at Albany Dance Hall 1940s. Eddie Lamb is on drums, with Bob Halford second from left, and Bob Carter on far right. (Jean Halford)

*We played quickstep, slow foxtrot, waltz, tango, rumba, and we used
to do a race. They would pick all the slow foxtrots from the top twenty,
and just play one chorus of each.*

*Everybody was dancing around and singing their hearts out because
they knew the tunes. At Cooke's we'd be working 7.30 in the morning
to 7.30 at night, and then you'd have thirty minutes to get home,
change into evening dress and get to the Albany. Dance bands played
a vital role particularly in a garrison town like York, with aerodromes
and camps springing up all around it. Where did they go? They caught
the bus into York and came to the dancehalls. Monday night was
medium, but the other nights were absolutely jam-packed. They'd be
queuing to get in.*

There were a number of canteens set up for members of the forces. Centenary Methodist Chapel in St Saviourgate, for example, had a canteen open every night from September 1939 onwards. They provided 1000-1200 meals a week for troops. There were a large number of volunteers willing to put in many hours there giving the troops a little bit of home comfort.

Rubye Readhead's mother was a volunteer there.

*And the volunteers used to invite the servicemen to come to their own
homes, because the thing they missed the most was their families.
We always had somebody there, soldiers or airmen, and it was lovely
because things like helping my younger sister to do her homework,
and simple things like making toast on the fire, made them feel more at
home. Our house* [in George Street] *was owned by the Tadcaster Tower
Brewery and the vehicles used to deliver there, and the foundations* [of
the houses nearby] *were sinking with the weight of the lorries. When
we had a party at Christmas, there was the Air Force men and the army
friends of my brother, and such was the force of the dancing that they
went through the floorboards in the front room!*

CONCERT PARTIES

ENSA (Entertainments National Service Association) was set up in 1939 to provide entertainment for the troops, and many performers, both professional and amateur, travelled all over the UK entertaining, and some even went overseas. Harry Warrington was a York pianist, who worked with Joan Pannett at the York Carriageworks, and he toured France in 1940 with George Formby's concert party.

Charles Barnard was a policeman during the war. He was a bass/baritone soloist and took part in concert parties, along with other musicians and conjurors.

> *We had a hell of a good concert party, believe me. We went to a couple of do's at the Empire. We went all over. Harrogate barracks was one place, and we had a real good do at Husthwaite Hall. There was an RAF*

Rowntree's concert party 1942. L to R – Kathleen Nutbrown (now Wilson), Joan Key, Audrey Kent, Betty Sturdy, George Watson (Rowntree's theatre manager), Jean Turpin, Betty Frost, unknown, Joyce Burnett. (Kathleen Wilson)

squadron stationed there. We had a mobile theatre and took a full show there, a two hour show. I used to sing opera as well as popular songs.

When I was in plain clothes, I'd come off at six and come home, the wife had some tea ready and I've packed up and collected it in my flask and the mobile theatre's been at top [of the street] waiting for me. I'd go in evening dress. We were policemen, or in the army or the RAF or one thing or another. We used to get some real ovations.

There were four of us. We had to get our chief's permission. He had a Rolls Royce and if there were three or four of us going to these outlying places, he used to run us out. When we went to Husthwaite Hall, all the bigwigs were at the front. It was full. When we'd finished, they gave us a supper in the mess. And one of them came to see me, and he said he did enjoy those songs. He said, "I've a brother who's died unfortunately, and he sang the 'Lute Player' that you sang tonight. That brought back memories, it really was great". And this Wing Commander walked out with me to the coach. He said, "By the way, just drink my health and my brother's, will you?" And he gave us a bottle of whisky.

In summer 1940 the City Police Concert Party presented 'a three hour concert in aid of Church Army efforts for troop comforts' featuring a 'masked mystery baritone' with songs from Mozart and *The Chocolate Soldier*, 'amusing yodelling' from PC Frank Lofthouse, comedian PC Fred Hirst 'who has the audiences splitting with laughter', his two sons on piano-accordion and Spanish guitar, (one being Bob Hirst who became a well-known York pianist), Stanley Holloway monologues, banjo playing, tap dancing and songs of the sea. The main feature was well-known local singer PC Bob Halford and his Embassy Band with 'up to date dance music'.

Audrey Halder describes how her mother, Elsie Hornby, took part in concert parties during the war. In April 1940, for example, she appeared

Molly Robinson, 2005
(Mike Race)

Molly Burley (later Robin-
son) playing accordion in
late 1930s
(Molly Robinson)

with Mrs Maher's Concert Party, who entertained the troops in the YMCA Hut at Strensall.

As a small child, Audrey herself sometimes went along with her grandfather, Elsie's father.

> *He made sure that she was safe. They had a bus and it was convertible into a theatre inside. They had a stage at one end and the audience could come in and sit down and watch the show, if there wasn't a*

*theatre or suitable venue at the air force or army bases that they went
to. Tommy Benson, of Benson's Bikes in Goodramgate, he played the
banjo, and there were a couple of sisters, Winnie and Margaret Maher,
they were singers. Harold Hatfield played the mouth organ and there
was a woman called Nancy Barrett who was known as York's Gracie
Fields. I remember going to one of the air force bases, and there was a
raid on, and they couldn't perform. Everybody just disappeared, went
to man the guns and everything and we were left in this hut, it was
quite scary at the time but everybody just laughed about it. It was the
Dunkirk spirit if you like.*

*I wish I still had my mother's dresses that she wore, the evening dresses
with sequins and all this. I mean they really were beautiful. My sister,
being a comedian, she wore a ballet dress and army boots or a Salomé
outfit with pan lids on as a bra. It was a variety show. Serious songs,
funny songs. 'We'll Meet Again', that type of thing. They were known
as the White Rose Concert Party, and they all wore a badge with the
white rose on.*

Molly Robinson was born in 1926 and from the age of 11, she performed
with an accordion band, the Six Minor Chords. During the war, she
graduated into being part of a concert party.

*We used to play at Rowntree's a lot and at the workhouse. We'd go
through the back and there was a table with a big jug of cocoa and a pile
of potted meat sandwiches. We couldn't be paid 'cos we were under age.
I joined the concert party because I could play accordion and piano. My
friend Betty used to sing. There was Bert the juggler who did magic, a
man called Reg ran it and his partner was the captain. He used to run on
in a ballerina's dress with a couple of tennis balls, and do a pirouette, and
tell jokes. We played at NAAFIs and village halls. We'd play at Linton
and Shipton by Beningbrough. One night we'd gone out to Shipton and
we met a woman who looked 16 but who had eight kids. But she could
whistle! So she joined in. It finished when some of them got posted.*

SPORT

Sport helped to keep up people's spirits and was good for morale. Soccer, cricket, rugby, fishing, horse racing, athletics, bowls, cycling and golf all continued in York over the war years. School sports were put on hold temporarily in the autumn of 1939, but then it was decided that they should continue, to give young people the necessary fresh air and exercise.

Bob Ferguson came to York from Middlesbrough. He had played football there for four seasons and was transferred to York in 1939. Football really attracted huge crowds. York City played at the ground in Bootham and during the war, the team constantly changed depending on where people were stationed.

We were getting about 9,000 down there at Bootham Crescent to watch matches on a Saturday, round about 1943,'44. There were that many people in the forces in and around York. And they'd nowhere else to go,

York City Football Club 1941-2. Bob Ferguson is 5th from left on back row. (Bob Ferguson)

so they went to the football matches. There was always players coming and reporting to Bootham Crescent. We had all sorts of stars coming down there to play, quite a lot of internationals who were stationed round here. We used to play all the top teams, Middlesbrough, Sunderland, Bradford and Leeds United. They'd all come to York. It was like a league.

HOLIDAYS AT HOME

One of the slogans during the war was *'Is Your Journey Really Necessary?'* The government discouraged unnecessary travelling, particularly by car, which would use up valuable petrol coupons. This meant that for the majority of people, holidays would have to wait until the war ended. Many towns and cities organised 'Holidays at Home', a series of activities over the summer period. York was no exception and a great many people took advantage of the events organised. In the summer of 1944, 'Holidays at Home' took place from 15th July to 13th August. There was a wide variety of events, including 40 concert parties, a number of dance and brass bands, talent spotting competitions, sheep dog demonstrations, donkey rides, Punch and Judy, marionette shows, classical concerts, and open air services. The Big Top marquee was erected on Bootham Stray with a special pitch-pine floor, and

space for 1000 dancers. Bands included the KOYLI band, (the King's Own Yorkshire Light Infantry), the Rifle Brigade Band, the RAF Six Wings and the Royal Canadian Air Force Overseas Bomber Group Band. Outside the marquee were a number of deckchairs and coloured umbrellas loaned by Great Yarmouth.

Big Top for Holidays at Home 1944 (York City Archives)

Holidays at Home, dancing in the Big Top, 1944 (York City Archives)

On the first Sunday of the month of celebrations, there was a grand choral concert by Monkgate Methodist broadcasting choir, an open air service with the Salvation Army band and the York City brass band. Six famous sheep dogs performed, including the 'film stars' Old Bob and Jeff! There were also cricket matches, demonstrations from the Yorkshire School for Alsatians, and a cavalcade of fashion and mannequin displays featuring 'fashions from the 10th century down to wartime utility vogues'. There were 18 boxing tournaments, open cycle runs by Clifton Cycling Club, gymkhanas and the Army School of Physical Training doing a demonstration. One of the highlights was Cody's Circus and Zoo, with twice daily performances on Knavesmire. Unlike modern circuses, they featured performing lions, dogs, tigers, horses and ponies as well as the flying trapeze. The other main highlight was the York and District Red Cross Agricultural Show on Rowntree's sports ground, with classes for horses, cattle, sheep, pigs, poultry and rabbits. There were also riding and jumping events.

By the end of 1944, 13,347 people had danced in the Big Top, eleven dance orchestras had entertained, 13,978 donkey rides had been taken by York children, in Acomb, Clifton, Hull Road Park, Leeman Road and Rowntree's Park. 3, 951 people had danced in the open air in four York parks, and over 2,000 had watched the sheep dog demonstrations. The villages of Haxby and Wigginton held their own concerts, displays of PT, films, bands, concert parties, and plays.

A 'Sports Gymkhana' was held at the York Rugby Football Ground, Wigginton Road, on Monday 7th August, which included military gymnastic displays, and all kinds of races for girls and boys, men over 45 and mothers. They obviously assumed that men under 45 would be involved in war work. As well as the usual obstacle, sack, three legged, skipping and slow cycle races, there were also the men's human barrow race, and the suspended apple eating competition.

The well-known Roosters concert party was formed by six army men in 1917. They went to Salonika, Greece, Egypt, Palestine and Jordan, offering 'gay army sketches'. During the Holidays at Home period, they performed every afternoon in Rowntree's Park, as well as evenings in Rowntree's Theatre, St Clement's Hall, Acomb Parish Hall and Tang Hall School.

Brenda Milner recalls,
> *At school they asked for volunteers to join the choir in St Helen's*
> *Square singing 'Land of Hope and Glory'. Very patriotic songs for*
> *part of the holiday week. York also had a very good repertory company,*
> *that went on through the war. There was a different play on each week.*

Instead of going for the cheapest seats, we decided to treat ourselves and get booked seats. And I remember one of my friends saying to the lady in the box office, "We've been potato picking you see. We can treat ourselves this week". In fact we did very well for concerts, with well-known orchestras, and famous people on the stage, because a lot of the theatres were closed in London. They just went on tour in the provinces. So we did see some of the really famous people.

Jean Cayley remembers

Gracie Fields came to Fulford Barracks to sing to the troops, and sat on the back of her car. Then there was a marquee in Bootham Park. I've danced in there all night long. Geraldo [a famous band leader] *set up a KOYLIs band with real tough fighting men.*

Jean Cayley 2005 (Brian Freeborn)

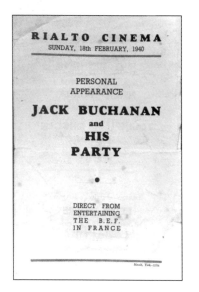

Occasionally there were concerts featuring top stars. Jack Prendergast at the Rialto had a lot of friends in showbusiness, and in November 1939, he engaged Jack Buchanan to appear with a number of West End artists.

Jack Buchanan at the Rialto 1940
(York Oral History Society)

CINEMAS

There were ten cinemas in York during the war. These were the Clifton, the Electric in Fossgate, the Grand Cinema in Clarence Street, the Odeon, the Picture House in Coney Street, the Regal in Piccadilly, the Regent in Acomb, the Rialto, Fishergate, St George's in Castlegate and the Tower in New Street. When the war began, all the cinemas were closed but they reopened on 9th September, as the government realised how important entertainment was at this time.

Picture House, Coney Street. 1940s
(York Oral History Society)

In August 1940, members of the forces and their companions were only charged 7d for seats, and 50% of the cinemas' accommodation was to be kept free for the forces.

Joan Sadler

liked the cinema. The Grand Cinema had double seats at the back and so did the Rialto. If anyone asked you out for a date, you could hold hands. Newsreels were always interesting because we didn't have television. Our 21st birthday (1943) [Joan was a twin] was spent seeing 'Watch on the Rhine'. I remember it well. We took some girls from work.

Ethel Jones was born in 1899. She and her mother came to York in 1941 when their house in Liverpool was bombed in an air raid. She had a married sister here and soon got work in the NAAFI office on Museum Street. She worked hard, often doing overtime until 7pm, but also enjoyed a good social life with lots of friends. Ethel kept a diary during the war. In August 1940 she spent a week in York with her sister, during which she went to Rowntree's Park, then for a sail up the river, to the Rialto to see 'Follow the Fleet' and the Theatre to see York Repertory in 'The Silver Box'. In 1941, once she had moved here, she mentions going to the Tudor Café, the Odeon, the Picture House in Coney Street, the Grand, St George's Cinema to see 'Kipps' and the Creamery Café. She also regularly visited the Rialto and went to a dog show in Delwood, Fulford, which is now all houses. On the evening of the York Baedeker Raid in April 1942, she went to see Fred Astaire and Ginger Rogers in 'The Story of Vernon and Irene Castle'. In the same month, she writes,

Ethel Jones, 1998 (York Oral History Society)

Had a walk to Heslington…saw 'Mrs Miniver' at the Regal…went to a whist drive…had tea at the Devonshire Café…then we saw 'Gone with the Wind' at the Regal.

On one particular Sunday, she records

Went to Bettys for lunch…then we walked to Bishopthorpe in the afternoon…went to the Theatre at night.

In June 1943,

We went to the Imperial Club auction sale for the Red Cross…had an afternoon off so went collecting for the blind…went to a garden fete at Gate Fulford.

Because Ethel was a single independent lady, she had enough money to spend on a decent social life. Her wage for the first week in September 1943 was £3.3s.3d, with overtime of 8s.7d, totalling £3.11s.10d, quite a good salary for a woman. Unfortunately her mother died on 14th September of that year, but she carried on with war work, helping her sister and seeing friends. She also began a weekly French lesson at Castlegate School. Ethel made the most of her time, enjoying life as much as she could. She lived to be 100!

Mary Beilby recalls,

> *They used to have lots of things going on in the Museum Gardens in the summertime. We'd go on a Sunday and there were often concerts there, and games for children. They put on teas too. The hospitium I think it was. Oh there was always something going on.*

A few families did manage to go on holiday, like Frank Jackson's, because his father worked at the York carriageworks.

> *We holidayed in Filey, 'cos my father had his railway passes. The only bit of beach you could get on was the Coble Landing. There was barbed wire everywhere, and troops. But the boats had to keep fishing.*

ROMANCE

Romance was important during the war, whether through personal relationships or through the escapism of films and love stories. There were so many new people in the city, and the opportunity to meet and dance with them was very exciting.

Winnie Mothersdale remembers

> *York was full of air force of every nationality. The Free French, the Dutch, the Poles who were very gentlemanly, clicked their heels and*

175

made you really feel you was somebody. I mean there was just little tiny star lights on the roads, and nothing in the streets, everywhere was pitch black but you could walk about quite freely and you never thought about anybody attacking you, raping or mugging you.

Olive Connell recalls the romantic music.

I listened to radio, Jack Payne, Henry Hall and Roy Fox, and all the old music. Well it wasn't old then was it? But I used to love to dance to it, I still love it. In winter, when I get my curtains drawn, I have a little jazz round, I think it's lovely.

Every Saturday night there was a dance in the Assembly Rooms. We all went in a crowd, and there was some lovely lads. There was never any 'doucy darcy' or anything like that, they were all good pals, they really were. But some of those Canadian lads, poor lads they got killed.

Wedding of Olive Towse and Ray Connell. St Maurice's, Monkgate 1945. L to R – Benny Connell, Ray Connell, Olive Connell, Doreen Towse, Mr and Mrs Towse. (Olive Connell)

Mavis Morton recalls

The first night I fell in love was the night of the air raid. Although we were always in a gang, we were virtually split up into twos. Our mothers were terrified, "You bring trouble and you're out". I don't think we realised what trouble was, we had no sort of sex education. It was, "Just keep away from boys". You hadn't to do this, you hadn't to do that. I wouldn't dare take a boy to our front door. But this lad walked me home, and then suddenly he pushed me on the floor and jumped on me. I said, "What's going on?" And he said he heard a bomb drop, it was less than a mile from where I lived. But I thought, if that boy would look after me, he must love me. Some of my friends, they married boys, it was probably the only man they ever had in their life. Don't think we never had feelings, we went through agonies. But a lot were devils during the war, some of these that had been married, they were on to a good thing, I knew a lot of this went on.

Doreen Varrie tells of her wartime romance.

I met Jerry, a French Canadian, on a blind date. He was a navigator stationed at Croft near Darlington. We went dancing mostly and to the pictures. He used to come back to our house a lot. It was a home for him. They were miles away from home, it must have been nice for him to stay with a family. I was 19. My Dad didn't like us out too late, but Mum and Dad liked him a lot. We used to go on trips on the river when he was available, or we would walk a lot. We went to the White Rose in Jubbergate and the Willow in Coney Street. They used to buy cigarettes at the PX Store. He used to get my dad Sweet Caporal, they were nice.

Doreen Varrie in 1950s
(Doreen Varrie)

If I'd have married Jerry, I'd have been equivalent to a G I Bride. We got engaged but some people resented them [Americans and Canadians]. One man saw my ring and said, "You should look after one of our own boys, not marry someone else". Even married women...there were quite a few illegitimate babies. The men were away and they were over here.

At the end of the war we were dancing in Parliament Street that night. I was happy. They didn't start demobbing them but we knew it wouldn't be long, they moved them pretty quickly. And he was making plans to get a house. He had a big family in Lachine near Montreal.

He went back. He wrote nearly every day and I got letters all the time. But I got cold feet. I didn't want to go to Canada. Jerry came back after the war, years after, in the '50s. I'd been married and divorced in between. Jerry had come over, all the way, flown into England, got a train to York, then a taxi. I wasn't there, I got a letter later saying I obviously didn't care enough. It was a bit of a blow. I didn't know he was coming.

A happier story was that of Rubye Readhead.

A group of us used to go out together. I was only 18, I'd never been to one of the big places to dance. One of the older girls said, "You teach me to swim and I'll teach you to dance". And it was working quite well. I got the waltz mastered and the foxtrot and I'm doing well with the quickstep. This particular day was Trafalgar Day, October, celebrating Nelson's victory. I wasn't very happy and I was sitting opposite the door in the De Grey Rooms, it was about 9 o'clock. The door burst open and there was a group of airmen burst into the room and the band was playing. And this airman

Rubye Readhead 2004
(Van Wilson)

came across and said, "May I have this dance with you?" And he was stationed at Linton on Ouse.

I'm a great believer in fate. The night I met him, they were going to go on a bombing mission to Dusseldorf. There was an American magazine Life, and the editor had got permission to go with the crew on an operation and they'd taken this photo of the crew walking out to the Halifax bomber. On this particular night, they were going across to get in the plane and a message came that the raid had been cancelled because of bad weather. So they piled into a bus and came into York. If the weather had been fair, I might not have met him. That was my husband.

Of course, wartime had its own difficulties,

My husband did three tours of operational duty. No-one knew where they were going, not supposed to know. Every night I used to hear the

Rubye Readhead (second from left) at brother's wedding, 1943 (Rubye Readhead)

bombers droning out over York. In the morning I'd get up for work and the bit I dreaded was, "Last night our bombers raided Cologne and five of our aircraft are missing". I couldn't settle at all, so he said, "I share a room with a New Zealander, we're not allowed to speak to anyone until we have been debriefed. But when we have I'll give him the number of where you work and you'll know then I'm back". That was a great thing to have. The only one time it didn't happen, they were coming back from a raid, they had to radio in to the nearest point, just off the coast and they got there safely. I didn't hear anything till teatime and I imagined him dead and buried, and the 'RAF March Past' [played at his funeral].

Rubye mentions another romance which came out of the York air raid.

A couple lived in Bootham Crescent and their parents were friendly with my parents, and next door to them was another young couple. And such is fate that when the bomb dropped, the wife of one of them was killed and the husband of the other. And in the end it had a happy ending because they married each other.

Some people blame the 'permissive' 1960s for the break-up of family life, but it is clear that the Second World War began the process. The enforced separation and loneliness took a huge toll on relationships, and both men and women sought comfort outside of their marriages. A common phrase at the time was 'Live for today for tomorrow we may die'. People grabbed at happiness where they could, often having to make quick decisions which were sometimes the wrong ones. Evelyn Hudson remembers

A girl I worked with at Kathleen Benson's, Gwen, she married a Canadian and about 1944, she went across to Canada as a war bride. And Rosie, she married a Polish airman. Two school-friends married Americans and went as GI Brides. I was bridesmaid for one of them. And she went, before the war finished, to America. But some of the poor lasses married GIs and thought they were going to the land of milk and honey and it wasn't. A lot came home heartbroken, but the people I knew that married foreigners seemed to have settled down all right.

A lot of the airmen that were stationed up here, quite a few girls went overboard with them and probably found out later on that they were either engaged or married, but there was some good romances.

I mean, you made a friend, and they were friends. He'd invite you to the dance, you'd have a good night kiss and probably not see him again for three weeks, but next time you went to the airfield he'd be there. Two of the lads that I knew, one was always called Woody, he was a Canadian, and the other Canadian was Richie. If they got chance for a weekend or even mid-week break, my mum used to put them up and we could go to the pictures or to a dance. But it was just a wartime romance, somebody to go out with, somebody to have a goodnight kiss with.

You could go to these different airfields for an evening's dancing and you'd meet somebody. I've heard girls say, "Ooh he was lovely. He's gonna write to me and I'll see him again", and then she'd probably see him two or three times and then, "Where is he? Have you heard?" Then next time you went, "Sorry, he didn't come back," so you more or less had to live for the day.

There was one lad who was in the navy and he was the first one that brought me a pair of nylons and some Max Factor make-up, and he used to take me out every time he came on leave and I used to go and see his mum. They lived at the corner of Nunnery Lane, and he badly wanted me to be engaged. He was a nice lad, I enjoyed his company but no spark, and he got quite upset, when I said, "No". At the end of the war he was in Australia with the navy, got demobbed and never came back, and as far as I know, never married either. His mum and dad went to Australia twice when they retired to have a holiday with him.

There were many tragedies too, like the account by Gwyneth Hopper about a recently married young airman.

I remember the aerodrome and the big planes coming in and the crews being billeted with people in the locality. We had numerous young men billeted with us because we had a spare room. I think my mother said she was paid something like 3/6 a night.

Of course these young men were full of life. We had Fleet Air men, they had a darker uniform than the RAF. I particularly remember their caps because they had the most beautiful badge on the front. It was like a crown and it was padded and scarlet and then gold, sort of wire over the top of this red padding. They were awfully nice too, I remember them saying, "I've got a sister just like you". If I'd been ten years older I think I would have had much more fun. Being about eight, I thoroughly enjoyed them. We had one very nice young man whose great friend was billeted just down the road with my friend's parents. He went to Doncaster as a favour to somebody and they ran into a factory chimney and he was killed. He'd just got married, his wife was a teacher at the local school. I gave him a tiny little teddy bear. It was about four inches long and had a little orange waistcoat with little knitted buttons and he called it Plumpy, and he had it in his aircraft. In exchange he gave me 'The Wind in the Willows', I've still got it. Inside it says, 'In exchange for Plumpy who I'm sure was a friend of Pooh and the people in this book'.

CHAPTER NINE
PRISONERS OF WAR

During the Second World War, a number of Italian and German prisoners of war were housed in camps around Britain. There were only two POW camps in 1939, but by the time the war ended the number had risen to over 600.

After the 1929 Geneva Convention, POWs were treated better than in previous conflicts and Red Cross parcels were sent to British POWs in prisons in Germany and Italy. Over 190,000 British men and women were imprisoned in German, Italian and Japanese prisons.

Eden Camp, near Malton, was the main POW camp in the York area, with several satellite camps, Sandbeds Camp at Brayton near Selby, Storwood Camp at Melbourne, Thirkleby Camp at Thirsk, and the camp at Naburn Hospital. There were also some prisoners at the Ministry of Food office at Amotherby. POWs were at Eden Camp from May 1942 to April 1948 and were housed 64 to a hut. Today the camp is a Second World War museum and has the most comprehensive and largest collection of prisoner of war information and artefacts in the world.

Prisoners at Eden Camp, chefs on front row (Eden Camp)

Although the Geneva Convention stated that POWs should not be forced to work whilst in prison, most Germans and Italians chose to work and this tended to be farm labouring, as well as working on the rebuilding of homes damaged as a result of air raids. The prisoners were given special bank notes as payment for their work. They could use these at the camp shop for stationery, toiletries and any food not on ration, but could not spend them outside the camp. Each note was stamped with the Eden Camp number, which was 83, changing later to 250. The Peacock family from a local farm, paid the camp for the prisoners' labour, and a receipt from 1943 for £11.14s.3d represented 141 hours at 1/8d an hour, plus four hours overtime at 2/11d.

The first inmates at Eden Camp were 250 Italian prisoners. They helped in the construction and extension of the camp, and Birch & Sons from York were the builders. German prisoners came later. The Italians left to go home in 1944 but most German prisoners stayed on for some time after the war, until 1948 in some cases. There were also those who never left, preferring to make their home in this country. On the whole the prisoners were treated well. They had books in their

Prisoner of War money voucher (Eden Camp)

German prisoners outside the huts at Eden Camp. Alfred Brandt is in centre of front row
(Eden Camp)

own language, English lessons, music concerts, films, and the opportunity to play sport. Some even produced their own newsletters with poems and articles. Eden Camp was used as a national model in terms of education and religion. The prisoners were mostly low security risk, including many Eastern Europeans who were used to agricultural labour. Prior to D-Day, many captured Germans were sent to Canada. These were mostly airmen and naval personnel, often officers. Having large numbers of prisoners caused problems with rationing, of course, because they had to be fed.

In her book on Eden Camp, Anne Jacques states that no-one really tried seriously to escape from the camp except for one occasion when an Italian prisoner made a bid for freedom. He had been refused the newly agreed two hour freedom which had been granted after the Italian forces had surrendered, in 1943. It was one of those 'spur of the moment' actions, he was unable to bear his captivity while his comrades left for a short taste of freedom. He tried to get under the barbed wire but became entangled and was discovered weeping over the hopelessness of the situation.

Prisoners were moved around to prevent 'escape gangs' forming. British staff also moved around and were usually men who were unfit for active service.

Whilst British prisoners in German camps were using paper to forge documents, and any other items they could, to try to escape, the Germans and Italians, in York at least, used anything which came their way to improve their surroundings and were not so intent on escape.

Arthur Cremer was a German prisoner of war, born in 1924.

Concert party performers at Eden Camp. Back row, 3rd from right is Aloise Plaiser, second from right is 'Moser' Barber. Far right on front row is pianist Helmut Mildner, Theatre director is on far left. (Eden Camp)

I turned up at Eden Camp in September '44. Italians had been there, they had built it actually with a builder from York, and we followed them up. It was well organised and could be made smart. We had a professor who was very clever and he did all the organising about the landscape and the garden. You wouldn't see a holiday camp as smart as that. But they treated us all first class. I was only 20 year old, though I was very cute at spying around, watching everything. I'd tip the boys off, I said, "Maybe you don't speak English, nor do I much, I only learnt it here". We never had English at school but soon I picked it up. In six months time I spoke better English than I do today because then I was just trying to speak the Oxford English.

I wrote plays and also produced them, each play lasting two and a half hours. There's still one there on the original paper that I wrote it on. I soon started organising things, "We need this, we need that". I used to do each play in about six different make-ups. I got help when I wanted anything sewn on such as wigs, (we took the part of women as well), and we had to have material to make dresses. And then I said, "We need plywood and stuff to make all the different figures and the platform, the stage outfits", and it was there.

Arthur was also able to secure the services of a German orchestra who were very popular.

Hitler used to worship them and he posted them to Jersey and there they played. One day I thought, "Well we need music as well here". Strange as it was, I got to the Commandant and tipped him off where this orchestra was. And we had them here within a fortnight!

We had a lot of boys that were handymen like joiners, cabinet makers, and they would start making toys and stuff for children. We were going out in groups to work and came back at nights and then we had a library there with German books. Boys that wanted to read could read, those who wanted to play, had their guitars. We made our own parties

Orchestra at Eden Camp (Eden Camp)

[at Christmas], *we had all the English soldiers in there as well. The Commandant saw we all got something, we had our own bakers, our own catering staff. They were a grand bunch of people. We weren't even particularly rationed, we were just like the army, we could have what we liked. We had our own place and football matches, but I worked hard. I was billeted out, but I often went back. In 1985 there was a camp reunion for those who remained in York.*

We had to be very careful, we were under strict observation as well, with sentries and that, guns always at the back, but we were very fortunate. We used to say, "Hey give us the guns, we'll clean them for you"! There was attempts to get out, I had a tunnel under the wire that nobody knew. We had two lads there who were both trained pilots, the old Junkers bombers, and they were the test pilots, they tested the machines first. They were crafty, they had arranged for us to escape once. The boys said, "Arthur, you do the operating on the radio, you speak English, and we do the flying and we clear off". Unknown to the Camp Commandant, we'd radio equipment, all with bits made

Letter sent from Romania to prisoner Wilhelm Roth (Eden Camp)

ourselves from farm lads we met, "Can you get us so and so?" "Oh yes, there's an old thing laid there, take that". And we built it up. They knew there was a radio, but they couldn't find it. But then I thought, "Boys, if we do get shot down by our own lads, we won't have it as good as we have it at the camp", and so we decided to stop.

We were only allowed about once a fortnight, a postcard, and once a month a letter, but we had freedom, and the British side, they was all good hearted.

Later on, Arthur went to Castle Howard and worked on the farm with land girls.

They were all nice, the land girls. They had a big hall where they did the corn drying, and on a lunchtime we had our lunch there, and the foreman would come out with a mouth organ and play, and we danced with the girls. The army engineers used to come to Castle Howard and practise there, and we were working in the fields and the army used to bring the boats across, and build bridges.

When I was first billeted out in October '46, I was first at Sheriff Hutton, looked after an 80-acre farm there, had only one boy, 15, and it was for a lady, she was 50, and her father was 85. They was running

189

this rented farm, and I looked after it. I'd had cavalry training, I was smart on horses. At Castle Howard I used to saddle the horses for George Howard's sister and then there was village shows. We were still in prisoner of war uniform. It was the same as the air force uniform, but all chocolate brown coloured, but it didn't bother me. They welcomed us wherever we went.

After the war finished, things changed a bit. We had freedom, our own bicycles and my own motorbike, a BSA 350. I always went back to the camp on Saturdays and Sundays, to see the theatre plays and football matches between local villages. Then the Land Army girls told me they had film shows on Thursday nights. When these boys came from America and stayed there, I made pals with one or two of them, and so I got one of them to join me, to help me out on the farm, and he made love to one of the girls so that they split up the farm and they sold it.

[In Germany] my mother had a smallholding, and the family there took in people from the Eastern side [Russia], and the house was always full. I thought, "I can't go back there, and be a burden". I lost a lot of money, I tried to get it back but I left it too late and couldn't claim anything. With the war lost, they lost all the books, so I had to start from scratch here. After the war I applied for nationalisation, I had to wait five years, and I got married in 1957.

There were also POWs on the Knavesmire. The main racecourse stand and other buildings there were converted into a detention camp, with barbed wire around it.

Naburn Hospital, on the outskirts of York, was opened as temporary accommodation by the Ministry of Health. One ward on each side was evacuated in 1942 for use by the military as part of the Emergency Hospital Scheme. The huts in the gardens were later used by prisoners of war. Gordon Fenwick lived near the camp.

In 1945 I moved to live at Naburn Hospital where my father was a charge nurse in the mental hospital and there was 15 cottages at the front. We had a lot of the searchlights about in Fulford. My dad used to have to do firewatching duty and had to go on the top of the tower at the hospital.

Gordon Fenwick, 2005 (Van Wilson)

I remember the prisoner of war camp. At the bottom of our garden which was roughly about 20 yards, was a coil of wire about a yard across, and then standard wire stretching from that. And it was all suspended from big telegraph posts for a height of probably 20 or 30 feet high.

The entrance to the camp was actually off Naburn Lane. There were some big gates and a very nice looking drive with ornate lamps down it. But it actually bordered alongside of that driveway, did the prisoner of war camp. And then round the back, were the kitchens. I think the prisoners probably cooked in there. As far as I can remember there was a mixture of Italians and Germans in there. The Italians had given up [in 1943] so they could wander about outside. They used to make wooden toys and pass them through the wire

Gordon Fenwick with friends and dogs outside Naburn Hospital, 1945 (Gordon Fenwick)

191

*on the end of a brush shaft, and foreign stamps, 'cos when we were
young it was the thing to collect foreign stamps. The toy I have is
actually a kangaroo and it hops down an incline of 30 degrees. And for
it to be able to do that, it's got to be weighted correctly and balanced
correctly, else it just wouldn't go. And it was probably carved with
a penknife or something. Or you got little boxes and little pecking
chickens that were on a drum with a weight on. So from the resources
that they had there, they were very clever. They had brown uniforms.
They said it was the English uniforms that were dyed brown and they
had a triangle on the back of it.*

*Wooden kangaroo made
by prisoners of war for
Gordon Fenwick
(Van Wilson)*

*A lot of the patients from the hospital were actually victims of the war.
They'd been in the front line, and it was very sad. But the hospital itself
was very interesting, it was self sufficient. There were two farms, one of
them kept the animals, the sheep, the pigs and the cattle. A dairy herd
obviously, they used to produce milk and the rest of them were slaugh-
tered for the meat for the patients. It had its own slaughterhouse which
obviously wouldn't be allowed nowadays with licensing, and they had a
butcher. And they had their own slue. They used to feed all the animals
on the leftover food from the hospital. Then on the other side they grew
vegetables and root crops. There was a staff of workers and the patients
seemed to do a lot of work on the farm.*

*They generated their own electricity and I was fascinated. I used to go
and see the generators they had, and the coal came for the boilers, and
that was taken up to the houses at the front, and the cost of the coal
knocked off people's wages. Our milk was unpasteurised and it went*

through a cooler. A patient came with a billycan on his shoulders every morning and put the billycan on the doorstep and that's how we got our milk. Plus they had a garden with an orchard and they grew flowers and everything for inside the hospital. The orchard is still actually standing round at the back of McArthur Glen.

Bill Denby lived on a farm in Heslington and he recalls

The German and Italian prisoners of war came to do the fieldwork. They used to travel by motor lorry. We had about ten Italians to hoe sugar beet and when they'd finished, they went back to the camps. Eventually it got to taking the potatoes up and we got a lorry load of 20 Germans and they brought their own food, made a camp fire and

Items made by prisoners of war at Eden Camp, clockwise from right, bread shoes, a chess set and cigarette case made from a mess tin with Lilli Marlene design. (Eden Camp)

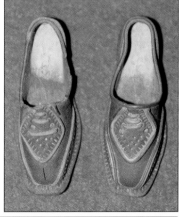

prepared their dinner round that. The Germans were good workers.
They picked potatoes into a basket and emptied the baskets into the cart.
They used to make a lot of carpets out of bands, they'd plait the string
they tied straw and hay bales with, and make slippers and sell them to
the housewives or anybody who would buy them. They used to make
rings out of shillings and sixpences.

The Italian and German prisoners were very good at handicrafts. They made a huge array of items, some practical and others for decorative value. There are many on display at Eden Camp, including musical instruments, model boats and planes, sculptures, paintings, ships in bottles and even one inside a light bulb, wooden toys, kaleidoscopes, Punch and Judy puppets, photo frames, cigarette cases and lighters, often engraved, ashtrays, bangles and rings out of wire and other metal, chess pieces and board, dolls' house furniture, collages from cigarette cards and rope slippers. There is a pair of miniature slippers made from stale bread rolled and painted. Apparently this was a common craft in Italy. There are also items with North African images, including mosques, painted on them.

Les Benson remembers a particular incident.

Later on in the war, my father was working on the airfields, he had
Italian prisoners of war helping him. And the lorry never come and
picked them up, so he messed about for an hour ringing up and couldn't
get any joy, so he got them out onto t'road, and these Italians started
tramping towards York. Service lorries weren't supposed to pick anyone
up but they gave them a lift right into Bootham. So me dad thinks,
"What now?" So he brought these six Italians home with him. They
all came into our house, so that 12 by 12 living room was absolutely
packed. We were sitting down and standing up. Then there was this
great knocking at the front door and the police were there and the army
police, looking for the Italians. And they all come trundling in, these
redcaps, they had a truck outside and they bundled them into that.

Some of them were lads not much older than me you know. That was all the rations gone, they'd eaten us out of house and home that night!

The Italians were popular in the area as they were full of fun, and were very friendly. They also had a bit of a reputation with the ladies. The Germans were more sombre but hard workers. Later in the war, prisoners went out for meals with local families, and even sometimes had days out at the coast with them. By late 1944, prisoners might be allowed out for 24 hours so they could share Christmas with a local family.

The prisoners were allowed to improve their surroundings by planting flowers and a vegetable garden. Some of the Germans built little castles (a mini version of those in Bavaria) on the lawn, as well as fountains. They were very talented.

The camps continued after the war. Britain was desperately short of agricultural labour in the late 1940s and rationing continued until 1954.

Jack Turner recalls the low security prisoners.

The racecourse was full of them. They marched from the station right down to Knavesmire with one Tommy at front and one at the back. There were Germans, and some Italians. They had a yellow patch on the back. Italian ones went to work. They used to work on the army dump off Tadcaster Road, and sit down by t'pond and have their snap. They used to weave baskets. None of them wanted to go back. We didn't bother too much about the Germans. They weren't fighting us, they didn't want any trouble.

I went potato picking when I was 12, where Tesco's store is, that was a field full of potatoes in 1941. You got half a crown a day and that was a fortune. He used to pick us up in a little pig trailer with a bit of straw.

He had a nice fancy Wolseley. They cut down on summer holidays and gave us three weeks in the October. One of the farmer's sons was in the army and he got leave to come back for that three weeks. And we tatie picked with German prisoners at Long Marston. We were in this field and a German prisoner of war was there, and one was sat with his cup of tea or 'drinkings' as they used to call them. The farmer's daughter came with a big pot of tea. One of the lads said, "Look what I've found", and it was a torch which was hand generated, no batteries. It must have been dropped by a German. I never ever saw one again.

Potato picking, 1943-4, Hutton Wandesley, nr Long Marston. Jack Turner is holding horse. (Jack Turner)

One man tells his own memory of POWs in York.

What should roll in onto St George's Field was two covered wagons and they were German prisoners of war. And I always remember because it was just before Christmas and it had been snowing. Lads being lads and Germans being the enemy, there was a lot of jeering. And Mr James, he came out of that hut, and he shouted at us and he made us all stand to attention and he gave us a right dressing down. He said, "Look, your dads or your uncles might be prisoners one day in Germany and would you like them treated the same way?" And everybody took notice of this. And all of a sudden these two wagon loads of German prisoners started to sing, and they sang Silent Night. And even to this day, when I hear Silent Night I always think of that. It just gets to me a bit.

CHAPTER TEN

THE PACIFISTS

In the First World War, those who did not join up to fight were given a white feather as a symbol of cowardice. When another world war began in 1939, there were many who were not willing to fight, and they risked not only the anger and hostility of others, but also in some cases dismissal from their jobs, and even imprisonment. Real pacifism was not an excuse to get out of fighting because clearly it came at a high price. There were, of course, different levels of pacifism. Some people were 'absolutists' who were unwilling to do anything remotely associated with war, and there were others who would not fight but would engage in occupations such as driving ambulances as a possible alternative. The Society of Friends or Quakers were closely allied with pacifism and the Quakers in York were very supportive to those who became conscientious objectors (or 'conchies' as they were called), and protested to the city council when they decided to dismiss any pacifist employees. By June 1940, 29 York Quakers had registered as C.O.s.

Tribunals which sat to consider the applications began in the autumn of 1939. The first was held in Leeds on 23rd October, and included several York men. The details were reported in the Yorkshire Evening Press. Kenneth Blanchard was a 20 year old Quaker, who said he believed that 'destroying human life is utterly incompatible with the will of God'. He said he was prepared to save human life as a civilian but would not 'agree to going into uniform to do so'. He said anything he did would be 'from a humanitarian point of view and not from an official government point of view'. He explained, 'I am willing to work on the land for food for women and children, but not to grow trees, as they could make wood for battleships'. The judge was quite tough in his questioning, but told Blanchard that he had courage to come and plead his case, and the unanimous vote of the tribunal was that he should be left on the register of conscientious objectors.

An Acomb man, Kenneth Brownless, aged 21, was also a Quaker and his father, a Methodist, had been a pacifist in the First World War. He said he had no objection to doing ambulance work with the Society of Friends Ambulance Unit. The tribunal also allowed him to remain on the register. A third York man, who was a nurse at a psychiatric hospital, was not willing to fight and felt that his work already involved helping others. But his name was removed from the register and he was told that he would be employed on non-combatant duties.

Eric A was a Quaker who held strong anti-war beliefs.

At the beginning of the war I was still in industry, which is where I started my working life as a young apprentice. I sensed that something was going to change as time went on. In my particular job I was distanced a bit from the developing programme of munitions and stuff for submarines and torpedoes. But it did creep in on us and along with three or four colleagues, I began to feel increasingly uncomfortable. After a bit it became quite clear to me that I couldn't stay in my particular job at that point in time. This was electrical engineering. It was clear that before very long a good deal of the time and energy of the business would be given over to, if not directly armaments, certainly war related issues. For a time my boss, who was very good, fixed me up in non-war work, pretty well anything from power stations to lamps, and I spent quite a bit of time on sound reproducer work. That kept me reasonably at peace in myself but it was temporary. The time had come when I was to withdraw, which I did.

If you were in a firm which was war-related, you were in a reserved occupation. I felt there was something quite unacceptable about this. I felt I was sort of in hiding and had to come out. My tribunal was very late in the war, 1943. I moved out of my normal job with the company and took on a lower level job to do with sound equipment for theatres. I felt at least it wasn't warlike. I slogged on at that for two or three years. I then felt that this just wouldn't do. So reluctantly I parted with the company.

*There were others, one chap moved out very quickly, he couldn't stay
any longer and he was top engineer. I undertook the change which
meant going back to the bench on a fitter's salary. But then for me it
did mean a parting of the ways which was very sad. I listened to a talk
given by one of the 'Friends', who were setting up the Friends Release
Service which operated on the home front. I ultimately found my way
to a tribunal for C.O.s and was allowed alternative service. I think they
were a bit soft on the Quakers actually. We had a much softer ride than
say Jehovah's Witnesses, they had a terrible time. I decided to push out
into full time membership of the FRS. That was in 1944.*

*The tribunal was in Birmingham, it was quite informal. You set out
your position and you added two referees and I got one from a chap who
had been a major in the First World War. He thoroughly disagreed with
my position but thought I was very sincere in holding it. And the other
was a member of the Meeting [Quakers]. There was a certain judge
who had a bad name and was quite harsh particularly to those who
took up the absolutist position. I was taking up the 'alternative service'
position. I was unwilling to take part in anything which had to do with
the promotion of war, I was willing at whatever price to readjust one's
life or work or family arrangements, to fulfil any reasonable request to
take over something which was perhaps of social importance, to do with
coping with some of the disruption which people in the country had
suffered.*

*I was willing to do ambulance work, which I did in my spare time.
Some were prepared to do nothing, not even prepared to fill in papers,
they would not cooperate at all. They landed very quickly in prison.
This wasn't the position I took. My request to take up work with the
FRS was, I thought, reasonable. I moved to London and came back on
occasions.*

*The FRS was pretty competent and it set up a vigorous and down
to earth operation in helping evacuees from London to get set up in*

various parts of the country which were relatively safe from air raids. It needed serving and organisation, buying an old house to set up as a refugee hostel, getting in supplies and equipping it, enough to hold 50 people perhaps crammed in, mostly women and children. It was quite taxing and I was at the servicing end of this for a time.

A good long preparation period took place, whether there was a chance of sending a relief team, for example, into Normandy, which the Quakers did. It was very small scale but training was well organised. It was crucial to set up a kind of team spirit and get to know each other and the language. Getting to know how to service vehicles, how to proceed on a bombed out city such as Le Havre which is where the French work first began. Another lot went into Czechoslovakia. You had to go in battledress but it had to be in Quaker grey. Now getting bales of Quaker grey in wartime! But Burtons had these thousands of yards and they were very quickly rolled up into dozens of battledress for men and women. It turned out to be a very important element of Quaker service overseas, because we were not confused with the military. In early 1946 I shot off to Germany. Coping with the thousands of conscripted workers from Poland, the Ukraine, from Russia, brought in by the Germans, serving mostly in huge work camps. The immense job of trying to cope with the displaced persons. A lot of conscientious objectors were in Catholic Relief, International Voluntary Service, Friends Ambulance Unit, Friends Relief Service. To look after these folk, feed them, house them, clothe them and above all try to preserve their integrity of life, to maintain the feeling that after all these terrible years they still mattered.

There is a dichotomy here, the iniquity of the Nazi regime which Friends knew about, because of their experience with the Jewish people and the highly organised programme of getting Jews out before the war which Friends and other churches had a hand in, they did know what a disaster it was. Our feelings were not anti-German. We felt it was utterly impossible to feel a personal hatred to German people, although of course we were terribly anxious about the results of the Hitler regime and all its evils.

The press reported instances of men who claimed to be C.O.s just to try to get out of joining the forces. Sometimes their pleas were rejected. The reason for acceptance of the pleas was often on religious grounds, as in the case of Frank Fox.

Frank Fox in the Auxiliary Fire Service (Frank Fox)

I had refused to register for military service and was supported at the tribunal by a letter from the manager of the optician's with whom I had worked closely for some time. He wrote, "I regret having to say this as an old soldier, but Frank Fox is quite sincere in his religious beliefs regarding military service". Mr. Justice Stable, who was later murdered by a man he had previously sent down for a criminal offence, ordered that I remain in my present employment of optician, until required for some wartime civilian service. I took a first aid course and was allotted to a first aid post. I did stints as firewatcher at three places.

I was ultimately instructed by letter at my home in Bradford to present myself at the Central Fire Station in Clifford Street, York, on 21ˢᵗ August 1941, to become a member of the AFS [Auxiliary Fire Service]. *I was very pleased to have been sent to do a civilian wartime service to the community which involved the possibility of danger to life or limb, without having to kill somebody.*

Frank Fox's story as an auxiliary fireman appears in the chapter on Civil Defence.

Ron Jeffrey was a committed pacifist but his plea was rejected as he was not particularly religious, even though he had some affinity with the Society of Friends. The tribunal took place in May 1940.

In the aftermath of the terrible First World War, it made a vivid impression on me to see ex-servicemen, maimed and unemployed, begging in the streets of York, trying to make a meagre living. I still remember one regular specimen who used to play records on a large type gramophone and after a shower of rain when the streets were quiet, the silence was suddenly broken by the strains of 'Roses of Picardy' rendered on a cornet by another maimed ex-soldier. It seemed unthinkable to me to have any more wars.

I was a pacifist right from the time I went to school. I attended Scarcroft Road council school from 1919, leaving at the age of fourteen. The strict method of teaching was, "Come out, the boy that doesn't know". If you got your sums wrong or made a spelling mistake, you got the cane. At a very early age I got the idea that it was wrong to have violence inflicted upon you and it was also wrong to inflict violence upon other people and that's perhaps how it was deeply ingrained in me not to take part in war. War seemed to me to be a criminal folly. There were anti-war films like '*All Quiet on the Western Front*', and '*Journey's End*', and I thought if there was another war, I would take no part in it, I would become a conscientious objector. It was quite a few years later that the Second World War broke out.

The PPU (Peace Pledge Union) met every Sunday afternoon in the Co-operative building and I joined it. It was initiated by a Quaker lady called Miss Mann and was kept going by her indomitable spirit. She must have written thousands of letters and her peace work had started from the First World War. The pledge was to have nothing to do with war.

Ron Jeffrey (Ron Jeffrey)

A conscientious objector's aim is not to get out of the war but to oppose it. As far as was humanly possible, I did nothing at all to help the war machine. I registered as a C.O. claiming absolute exemption. I was sent to a tribunal in 1940. I felt that it was mentally, morally and psychologically impossible to accept any decision of the court that did not allow me exemption. I had to appear in Leeds in front of Judge Stewart who was notorious for making remarks about 'conchies' being cowards. He did offer me hospital work or work on the land alternative to joining the army. My peacetime occupation was driving a van for food distribution and I wanted to do nothing whatsoever to change my occupation. This was an important principle for the absolute conscientious objector – they would not accept any condition of getting out of military service. What usually happened was that they got impatient

*with anyone recalcitrant and they were struck off the register and liable
for full military service. There was an appeal held in York and I had
to prove that I was not a coward and had to face the consequences, of
going to prison. In September 1941, I was sentenced to six months in
prison and a fine of £25. If I didn't pay the fine, I would get another
three months.*

*PC Simpson took me to York station and we got on the train, a one way
ticket for me, and I got my first taste of prison in Armley Jail. You had
the first fortnight in a cell in solitary confinement with no mattress and
hard labour. They had put me down as 'fit for quarry work'. The first
thing every prisoner does is to look through the bars to see what the
view is like and I remember looking at this dirty, smoky town as it was
then, and that was looking at life through prison bars. They say that
'stone walls do not a prison make nor iron bars a cage', but it wasn't at
all fun being a conchie in wartime. After a few weeks at Armley I was
transferred with more C.O.s to Wakefield. I was handcuffed to a fellow
prisoner who had been violent to a policeman, he had hung him up by
his cape on a lamp-post. One of my first memories was that the deputy
governor there was a Quaker, and whether he had a softer attitude to
conchies I am not sure, but he asked me to black out the prison. But I
was going to have no truck at all with ARP [Air Raid Precautions]
arrangements. It may sound extreme but that's how I felt about it and
he didn't pursue the matter further. During 1941 and '42, the punishment cells of Wakefield Jail (where you got bread and water instead of
the usual diet) were full of those who refused to do war work, this in
some cases would be stitching blankets to be used in the armed forces.
I wasn't offered this work, but kept to stitching mailbags, but still got
the same diet, the usual two or three days loss of remission. I got this
for refusing to take part in gas mask drill. I never wore a gas mask
throughout the war.*

*I was taken on by a shop in Walmgate called Beaumont's. That's the
job I did before I went into prison and when I came out. By that time*

*rationing had got so acute they didn't need anybody to take bread out.
They had to queue up for it and were lucky if they got much of it. For
several months, I went round different farms and I went to Melbourne
and Sheriff Hutton, but not as an alternative to military service. I
was freelancing in farm work all over the country until the authorities
caught up with me. I had to go to the labour exchange and tell them
what my position was and they said, "You can get three months for
that", and I said, "I don't mind. I've just done nine". So I carried on
working and then I thought of the Friends' mental hospital called the
Retreat, and I wrote to ask if they wanted a porter, and they took me on.
The Friends' Retreat at York was one of the first mental hospitals in the
country to carry out humane treatment of the mentally ill. Before that
it was thought that madness or nervous breakdowns could be treated
by violent punishment, beating them up to get the insanity out of their
systems. A Quaker called Tuke and a few more like-minded people had
totally different ideas. They treated them with great sympathy and kind-
ness, by occupational therapy, medication and other humane methods
and above all a great atmosphere of friendliness which pervaded the*

The Friends' Retreat (Lesley Collett)

Retreat and was immediately obvious to me when I worked there. Everyone seemed to be trying to be nice to each other. Of course this suited me down to the ground. Here I was, wanting nothing to do with the war and the Retreat was a private hospital treating private patients, using humane treatment instead of violence. What more could I ask? As a porter I did all sorts of jobs, cleaning windows, polishing floors, taking the post round, going round the wards emptying the rubbish and taking some to the incinerator. There I was trying to make myself useful, willing to do anything.

I was fully expecting to be called up again but I never was, I received complete exemption from military service despite the verdict of the military tribunal. But it was more luck than arrangement. When the war ended they asked me to stop on at the Retreat and I later became a hospital warden and spent nearly ten years there.

CHAPTER ELEVEN

THE END OF WAR

WHERE YORK MADE REVELRY

The De Grey Rooms was the centre of York's VE celebrations. Dance music was relayed to vast crowds outside the hall (Yorkshire Evening Press)

By late 1944, the threat of invasion was over, and the strict regulations, including the blackout, were relaxed. On 7th September, the Yorkshire Evening Press reported "York welcomes blackout relief". Two days later, 122 evacuees returned to London. York still had 2213 official refugees. On 16th September, the Press reported that another 440 evacuees had returned to the London area, and during that week 296 more returned. But then a new problem reared its head, and there was chaos in London when the V2 flying bombs began coming over from Germany. 144 evacuees came back to York. So the situation was somewhat fluid. The government declared that they would not repay any fares to London as they did not want a big influx going into the capital. The other problem was the schools. Some were no longer there, having been destroyed in the blitz, and others were full, so there were no places for returning children. But by the beginning of 1945, the V2 flying bomb launch sites had been destroyed and the end was in sight. The number of evacuees quickly dropped again. Civil Defence was not such a priority and in December 1944, the Home Guard was officially stood down.

The end of war finally came on 8th May, VE Day. The BBC Home Service broadcast a programme of celebration, including Winston Churchill from 10 Downing Street, the victory bells, the BBC Symphony Orchestra, an interview with General Eisenhower in the USA, Lew Stone's dance band in Southampton, live music and conversation from various parts of London. During the afternoon, victory bells sounded from London, Liverpool, Cardiff, Edinburgh and from York Minster.

The dancers in York were out in force in the first week of May, with the Assembly Players at the Folk Hall, New Earswick, the Ambassadors at the Albany, the Metronome Dance Band at Copmanthorpe Village Hall, Bert Keech and his band at the De Grey Rooms, and other dances at the English Martyrs Hall, Clifton Cinema Ballroom, the Co-op Hall and the Dunnington Reading Room. There was a dance at the York and District Anglo-Polish Society in aid of Polish Relief, at the Rechabite Hall, and a dance at Acomb Parish Hall in aid of the RSPCA.

On VE night itself, there was dancing at the De Grey Rooms with the York Branch of Commonwealth from 8pm-12am, to Jack Carr's Melody Aces at the Co-op Hall, a VE Dance at the Clifton Cinema Ballroom, and a Victory Ball at the Albany from 8pm to 1am with the Ambassadors. The De Grey Rooms hosted a Grand Victory Dance with Bert Keech and his band on the following night, which was called V E Day + 1.

Rowntree's victory greetings, 1945
(Yorkshire Evening Press)

WP Brown's celebrate VE Day 1945
(Yorkshire Evening Press)

The village of Cawood had a 'Welcome Home Fund' in 1945. They had been saving for months to afford to hold celebration events for the end of the war. Many areas in York held street parties. Frank Jackson lived on Knapton Lane where there were a number of business people. One of the big houses hosted the VE Day party, as he recalls.

He was Newbald Kay, the solicitor. We had races, and everybody took part, and we had fancy dress. I had an Indian's costume, I'd had it a long time. My elder brother David was a Chinese man. The mothers would be able to use sewing machines and adapt other clothes.

Frank Jackson, 2005
(Van Wilson)

209

VE Day party in Knapton. Frank Jackson is second from right, his brother is far right. (Frank Jackson)

Gwyneth Hopper was nine when the war ended.

> *I remember clearly John who lived in Malton Way, my friend, he came round and he said, "The war's over". I said, "I don't believe you". He said, "Yes it is, I know it is, 'cos my mum's crying". And I couldn't wait to see the bunting in the street. I remember flags being put out and I remember my Granny taking me down Rawcliffe Lane to see the houses lit up. I was so used to blackout, I had never seen different coloured curtains and I thought it was like fairy lights, I was so thrilled with it.*

Doreen Angus describes the evening of VE Day.

> *There was a great celebration that night. I remember this friend in Haley's Terrace, putting the flags out of the window and then we went*

into town and for a drink to the George Hotel, which was across where Stonebow is. I remember meeting a lot of friends and coming back with arms linked and singing and doing the Palais Glide all the way home.

Alwyn Banks also enjoyed the evening.

For VE night, being an electrician, another job I was given, we had a lot of coloured lights in store through wartime and they were in a room over a sub-station in Walmgate. I was in charge of some apprentices and I set up a test bench and we tested 6,000 coloured bulbs and all the strips. Before VE night, they put the lights down the middle of Parliament Street up on the lamp posts and also in the trees opposite the De Grey Rooms. All the people were out and everybody was laughing and dancing, and to have the church bells and all these coloured lights, it was quite a display, it was lovely.

VE Day in Knapton, 1945 (Frank Jackson)

Mary Barnes recalls

> *At the end of the war. there was a feeling of hope, it was over, there*
> *wouldn't be any more wars, and everything in the garden would be*
> *lovely. And the troops when they came home would be housed properly,*
> *there would be jobs. As we all know, it didn't materialise and that sort*
> *of feeling of hope gradually diminished.*

Although everyone was very glad that the war was over, the economy was in a bad way, and a lot of people suddenly lost their jobs. For women this was particularly difficult, as they had grown used to independence, and the knowledge that their contribution was vital. The 1950s would be a period when the prevailing ideology was to get women back into the home. Although the new Labour government brought in the NHS and nationalised industry, the post-war period was grim in this country and it would take time to rebuild.

The years 1939 to 1945 had changed our society, and one thing was certain, things would never be the same again. The war had been a difficult and destructive time, but the majority of people had worked hard to pull together and fight in whatever way they could to defend their homeland. The armed forces, those involved in civil defence, the children torn away from their homes, those who 'kept the home fires burning' suffering huge restrictions, with the fear of loss and death never far away, had all played their part. Some of them are represented in this book, which, by recording their individual stories, is an attempt to acknowledge the debt we owe to each and every one of them.

Profiles of the Interviewees

DOREEN ANGUS was born in York in 1923. She went to work at Rowntree's in 1939 and also acted as an ARP messenger in the evenings, before joining the Women's Land Army in 1942.

AVRIL APPLETON came to York in 1939 as an evacuee from Hull, when she was five years old. Avril talks about this, as well as rationing and rabbit pie suppers when everyone 'did a turn'.

ALWYN BANKS was an electrician for the York Corporation and was in charge of air raid sirens and electricity in public shelters in York. He later joined the RAF.

GERALD BARKER was born in York in 1930 and was evacuated to Canada for the whole of the war, from the age of nine to fifteen. As an adult, Gerald ran his own hairdressing business.

CHARLES BARNARD was born in Sheffield in 1911, and came to York when he was eight. He was a policeman for most of his life. As a bass/baritone soloist attached to Northern Command, he sang in concert parties all over the district. He died in 2005.

MARY BARNES was born in 1912 and worked as a solicitor's secretary. She was an ARP warden during the war.

MARY BEILBY came from Lincoln to become a matron at Newburgh Priory with three schools of evacuees. She married and came to York and worked at the Ministry of Labour in the department for women's employment.

NICK BEILBY, her son, was born in the 1950s, and talks about his father, Robert Beilby, who worked at Handley Page aircraft factory at Clifton.

LES BENSON was born in 1928. He worked at Barnitt's store before joining the RAF as a regular for 12 years.

PETER BINNS was nine when the Baedeker Raid demolished his house in Lavender Grove, Poppleton Road in April 1942. Before the raid, he had felt that the war was a bit of an adventure, but after that event, realised the seriousness of it. Peter worked for many years for York Radio Relay.

JOHN BIRCH was born in 1922 in the Holgate area, and was in the Home Guard at the gas company, and remembers air raids and the guard room being demolished. He went into the Marines in 1943 and was out in the Far East until 1947.

DOREEN BOLTON was landlady of the Royal Oak in Goodramgate. Born in York in 1910, she was part of a family dynasty of pub owners in the city. She died in 1996.

EILEEN BROWN was of Irish descent and was born in York in 1914, and lived in the Walmgate area for most of her life. Her father was very involved in the cattle market. During the war, she was a driver at the station and remembers taking bodies to the mortuary.

MOLLIE CAFFREY was born in 1927 and came to Elvington as an evacuee from Sunderland and stayed on after the war, working in Pocklington and marrying a local man.

CISSIE COLLEY was born in Bishophill, York in 1910, one of twelve children. By the age of 18 she had to leave home because she had a serious boyfriend, Fred Colley, who she married a few years later. Despite living in lodgings, she had to give her mother part of her wage. She spent her working life at Terry's.

OLIVE CONNELL was born in 1919. Her aunt ran the Black Swan public house in Peasholme Green, where she often helped. Both her brother and husband were dance band leaders in the city.

ARTHUR CREMER was born in Germany in 1924 and came to Eden Camp near Malton as a prisoner of war at the age of 20. He stayed in York after the war.

WALTER DAVY was a boy during the war. He enjoyed music, particularly that of the dance and jazz bands of the 1940s and '50s. Walter worked in telecommunications for the railway, and went on to be parts manager at several York garages. His older sister is Doreen Varrie.

NANCY DAWSON was born in 1922 and worked at Rowntree's making munitions. Later in the war she joined the ATS.

BILL DENBY was born in 1906 and worked in a reserved occupation on his family farm. His wife, NORA, was also from a farming family. She was born in 1905.

JOYCE ELLIOTT was born in York in 1926, and her sister JEAN CAYLEY in 1928, two of five sisters. They have lived in Bootham since early childhood. They talk about the canteen at York Station, prisoners of war, foreign troops in York and dances.

LILIAN FAULKNER was born in 1915, and worked briefly as a telephonist for the Fire Service before going into the Land Army. Her husband was in the army but was killed in Italy. She later married for a second time.

GORDON FENWICK was born in Stillingfleet in 1942. His father worked at Naburn Hospital and he remembers the Italian POWs at the camp there. The hospital was self sufficient and had two farms which produced milk, meat and vegetables.

BOB FERGUSON worked at Cooke, Troughton and Sims in Haxby Road, making tank periscopes. He was in their branch of the Home Guard, and was a semi-professional footballer, playing in the wartime football league.

FRANK FOX became a conscientious objector at the start of the war. He came to York from Bradford to join the Auxiliary Fire Service, and was involved in the Baedeker Raid on the city.

SHEILA GOATER was born in Bootham in 1923. She attended the Bar Convent and later went to Leeds University. She taught in London before returning to York. After the war she married PETER, who was also born in York. He worked for Cooke, Troughton & Sims. They recall the air raids, the Home Guard and the aerodromes around York.

PHYLLIS HADDACKS, whose story is told by her daughter Lois Wilson, was a domestic science teacher at Scarcroft School. She was fire watching there on the night of the Baedeker Raid.

AUDREY HALDER was born in 1934. Her mother, Elsie Hornby, sang professionally in the 1920s to '40s, and appeared in York Light Opera and wartime concert parties.

EDNA HALL came from Sutton in Ashfield and lived in York for part of the war. Her son ROBERT, who became a surgeon, talks about his father who was in the Medical Corps and worked at the Military Hospital, before going into the Army Education Corps.

EUNICE (UNA) HISCOE was born in York and worked at Handley Page aircraft factory on Clifton aerodrome, in the canteen office.

KATE HOUGHTON was born in Trinity Lane in 1927. She went to Mill Mount Grammar School and later worked as a teleprinter taking messages for aerodromes. She described the war years as being a special time in her life.

EVELYN HUDSON was born in Kirby Wharf in 1926 and went into the Observer Corps from 1943, working underground near the Knavesmire.

CHARLES HUTCHINSON was born in Stillington near York in 1925. He was a full-time musician for most of his life, but was in Burma with the army during the latter part of the war.

FRANK JACKSON was born in 1938 and talks about being a young child during the war and the VE Day party at the end.

RON JEFFREY was born in Bishophill in 1915. After witnessing the maimed and unemployed soldiers from the First World War, begging on the streets of York, he vowed never to have any involvement in war. As an absolute pacifist, he was sent to prison but later worked at the Retreat hospital.

TONY AND MAUREEN JERRUM were children during the war, and recall having evacuees to stay with their families, Tony in Haxby and Maureen in Huntington. Tony also had airmen billeted on the family.

ETHEL JONES was born in 1899, and moved to York from Liverpool when her house was bombed in 1941. As a single woman, working for the NAAFI in Museum Street, she enjoyed a reasonable social life, and was a regular visitor to the theatre.

MAURICE KERSHAW was born in 1900 and worked at Rowntree's for his whole life. He was in charge of the munitions department and describes this dangerous but very important work.

EDDIE LAMB was born in Hull in 1922 and came to York in the late '30s. He worked for Cooke, Troughton and Sims in the Aeronautical Inspection Department, but later became a professional musician.

JOHN MCELHERAN was born in 1929 and attended Archbishop Holgate's Grammar School. His father was music master at the Yorkshire School for the Blind and organist at St Michael le Belfrey Church. He remembers the air raid in 1942. Mr McElheran died in 2005.

JOHN MENNELL was born in Orchard Street in 1926, and was an ARP messenger at the time of the Baedeker Raid and helped to save some nuns from the Bar Convent. He later went to the Middle East with the RAF.

BRENDA MILNER was 13 in 1942. Her father William worked at the station and was killed on the night of the Baedeker Raid. He posthumously received the King's Commendation for Gallantry.

CHARLES MINTER was born in 1897 in Kent. He joined the Navy in 1915, moved to York in the 1930s and was appointed City Engineer in 1935.

WINNIE MOTHERSDALE was born in York in 1912, and worked at Terry's during the war on aircraft propellers. She recalls being trapped when her house was destroyed in the Baedeker Raid.

JOAN PANNETT was born in 1919 and worked at York Carriageworks for the whole war, inspecting parts being made for Botha aircraft which were manufactured in Hull.

CHRISTINE RAYSON was born in 1924, attended York College for Girls and worked for the Knights of St Columba in Stonegate, employed by the Canadian government to look after the needs of Canadians in the forces. Her husband ERIC RAYSON recalls rationing and food clubs. He was in the army and spent most of the war overseas.

RUBYE READHEAD was born in York in January 1924. She worked in the NAAFI and then the Civil Service. She married an RAF squadron leader during the war.

LILIAN ROBERTS was born in 1913. She enjoyed going to the Empire theatre and the cinema during the war, as well as looking after her family.

MOLLY ROBINSON was born in York. She played in a young people's accordion band and talks about entertainment during the war.

MABEL ROBSON was born in 1907. Her husband was in the Home Guard and did firewatching at the Station Hotel until he was called up in 1941 and was sent to the Far East.

JOAN SADLER was born in 1922 and attended Priory Street School, then went to work at Rowntree's. She talks about entertainment and her working life.

JOHN SCOTT came to York from Newcastle in 1941 when he was 13. His father was in the Home Guard and later worked on the railway. He recalls the air raids.

JACK SMITH was born in 1910. Most of his life was spent working on farms, including forestry on Lord Deramore's estate in Heslington.

JACK & KEITH TURNER are brothers born in Leeds in 1930 and 1936. They moved to York in 1937, and talk about life as children during the war, air raids, and memories of their father's work in the railway offices.

DOREEN VARRIE was born in 1925, and during the war she was a van driver for the Maypole Dairy in High Ousegate. She recalls the unofficial billeting of people, and also talks about her romance with a Canadian airman.

MILDRED VEAL was born in 1922 in Hull, and went to train in Durham with the ATS in 1941. She was posted to Oswestry to work on a searchlight battery, on Ack Ack guns. Although women never actually fired the guns, they were involved in the setting up and preparation.

JOHN WAITE was born in 1923 in St Saviour's Place. He recalls scrambling across the roofs of St Saviourgate to put out incendiary bombs.

HAROLD WELBURN was born in York in 1931. He recalls helping Irish Navvies build air raid shelters and going on a fire training course. He witnessed the air raid on the Groves area of the city.

STAN WELLS was born in 1911. He worked as a taxi driver and then policeman during the war. His wife JOYCE WELLS worked for the Ministry of Food.

SHEILA WHITE was born in 1925 and left school at 14 to work at Rowntree's. She was also a volunteer two nights a week on one of the wards at Naburn Hospital, which had been taken over by the military.

ROSE MARY WILCOX was evacuated from Leeds to Pateley Bridge at the age of five. She recalls the transition from town to country life as an evacuee, including going to school on a shire horse.

GEORGE WILSON was born in Osbaldwick in 1903. He worked at the Elvington aerodrome during the war and recalls both the English and Free French air force squadrons based there.

ANTHONY WOOD was born in Strensall in the house next door to the golf club, in 1931. His father ran the business T F Wood and Co in Skeldergate. He remembers air raids, life in Strensall when troops came, and going to school at St Olave's.

ACKNOWLEDGEMENTS

In any work of this nature, there are always a number of people whose help and support have been invaluable. I would like to thank the following personnel of York Archaeological Trust : Mike Andrews for copying photographs; Lesley Collett, Graphics Officer, for scanning photographs and the design and layout of the book; Andrew 'Bone' Jones for the original concept of the Home Front Recall project; Sarah Maltby, Director of Attractions, and Chief Executive, John Walker, for their support.

We would particularly like to thank those organisations who have helped to fund this project: Friends of York Archaeological Trust, Sheldon Memorial Trust, Patricia and Donald Shepherd Charitable Trust and the Yorkshire Architectural and York Archaeological Society.

I wish to thank Rita Freedman, City Archivist, and the staff of York City Archives, staff of York City Reference Library, local historian David Poole, and York Oral History Society for allowing me to use some of their interviews and photographs. Nick Hill, Museum Director of Eden Camp, very kindly allowed us to use some of their photographs, and provided details of the history of the prisoner of war camp based there.

Thanks are due to the Friends of York Archaeological Trust who helped out in the process of interviewing and transcribing recordings : Barrie Ferguson, Brian Freeborn, Peter Harrison, Joyce Miller, Monica Nelson, Su Wompra.

Special thanks must go to fellow oral historian Mike Race, for help with research, copying photographs and for reading the final text and making useful comments, and to Christine Kyriacou, Archivist at York Archaeological Trust, for her support and encouragement, and her painstaking work proof-reading and checking the manuscript, and for her helpful suggestions.

Most of all, I want to thank all those who have allowed us to record their memories, and copy their photographs. They appear individually in the list of profiles.

BIBLIOGRAPHY

BROWN, Mike   *Put that Light Out : Britain's Civil Defence Services at War.*
                         Sutton Publishing, 1999

HARRIS, Carol   *Women at War 1939-45, the Home Front*
                         Sutton Publishing, 2000

JACQUES, Anne   *Eden Camp: the People's War 1939-45*   Eden Camp, 1997

PARSONS, Martin &
STARNS, Penny   *The Evacuation : the True Story* DSM, 1999

ROWNTREE & CO   *The Cocoa Works in War-time 1939-45.*
                         Rowntree & Company Ltd., 1947

RUBINSTEIN, David   *Faithful to Ourselves and the Outside World : York Quakers during
                         the 20th Century* William Sessions, 2002

WHITING, Charles   *Fire Over York*
                         GH Smith, 2005

YORK CITY LIBRARY   *York in the Second World War* 1992

YORK CITY OFFENCE BOOKS 1939-45

YORK COUNCIL MINUTES 1937-1946

YORK REFUGEE MINUTE BOOK 1939-41

YORKSHIRE EVENING PRESS 1939, 1940 and 1945

OTHER BOOKS BY THE SAME AUTHOR

The History of a Community: Fulford Road District of York.
University College of Ripon and York St John, 1984

Alexina: A Woman in Wartime York. Voyager Publications, 1995

Rich in All but Money: Life in Hungate 1900-1938. York Archaeological Trust, 1996
(Revised edition 2007)

Beyond the Postern Gate: A History of Fishergate and Fulford Road. York Archaeological
Trust, 1996

Humour, Heartache and Hope: Life in Walmgate. York Archaeological Trust, 1996

York Memories. Tempus Publishing, 1998

Number 26: The History of 26 St Saviourgate, York. Voyager Publications, 1999

Voices of St Paul's: An Oral History of St Paul's Church (Edited). William Sessions, 2001

*Rhythm and Romance: An Oral History of Popular Music in York. Volume 1 : The Dance Band
Years.* York Oral History Society, 2002

*Something in the Air: An Oral History of Popular Music in York. Volume 2 : The Beat Goes
On.* York Oral History Society, 2002

The Walmgate Story. Voyager Publications, 2006